Pat Sloan and Jane Davidson

The Splendid Sampler 2

Another 100 Blocks from a Community of Quilters

Martingale®
Create with Confidence

The Splendid Sampler 2:
Another 100 Blocks from a Community of Quilters
© 2018 by Pat Sloan and Jane Davidson

Martingale®
19021 120th Ave. NE, Ste. 102
Bothell, WA 98011-9511 USA
ShopMartingale.com

Printed in China
23 22 21 20 19   8 7 6 5 4 3 2

Library of Congress Cataloging-in-Publication Data is available upon request.

ISBN: 978-1-60468-952-5

MISSION STATEMENT

We empower makers who use fabric and yarn to make life more enjoyable.

CREDITS

**PUBLISHER AND
CHIEF VISIONARY OFFICER**
Jennifer Erbe Keltner

CONTENT DIRECTOR
Karen Costello Soltys

DESIGN MANAGER
Adrienne Smitke

MANAGING EDITOR
Tina Cook

PRODUCTION MANAGER
Regina Girard

ACQUISITIONS EDITOR
Amelia Johanson

COVER AND INTERIOR DESIGNER
Kathy Kotomaimoce

TECHNICAL EDITOR
Nancy Mahoney

PHOTOGRAPHER
Brent Kane

COPY EDITOR
Sheila Chapman Ryan

ILLUSTRATORS
Lisa Lauch
Sandy Loi

CONTENTS

INTRODUCTION

Welcome to our worldwide quilting community!

When we started the Splendid Sampler Sew-Along on Facebook, we had no idea it would become such a special place for quilters to share their creative lives. The experience has been astounding—80 designers, more than 28,000 quilters, and 100 quilt blocks to enjoy.

When *The Splendid Sampler* was published it became an instant best seller, spurring even more quilters to sew, share, and offer ideas and support. The Facebook group exploded with amazing blocks, each one more beautiful than the next. The designers shared their stories, and quilters like you added theirs. The group has become a melting pot of friendship, education, and inspiration. True beginners, seasoned quilters, and everyone in between sews alongside each other, cheering each other on.

It's been an incredible journey. We simply didn't want it to end! That's why we decided to invite *another* 80 designers to join us for *The Splendid Sampler 2.* We asked them to create a block in their signature style that answered this question:

I'm living my best quilting life when . . .

This talented group of designers will inspire you with their answers. And we can't wait to see and hear yours!

In *The Splendid Sampler 2,* we kept the size of all 100 blocks to 6" again, just like the first book, so you can combine blocks from both books and stitch your own story. As you'll see throughout these pages, there are many more gorgeous blocks to create and many more heartfelt stories to be told.

So, whether you're new to *The Splendid Sampler* or you've been following along since day one, get ready to get social with the Splendids! Check your favorite quilt shop to see if they're hosting a sew-along, join the community on Instagram (#TheSplendidSampler), show off your blocks on our Facebook group (facebook.com/groups/TheSplendidSampler), or visit our website (TheSplendidSampler.com). We can't wait to see you!

~ *Pat & Jane*

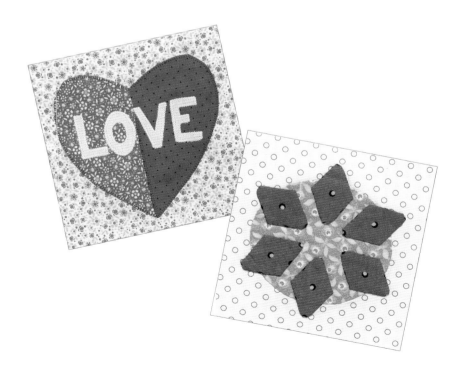

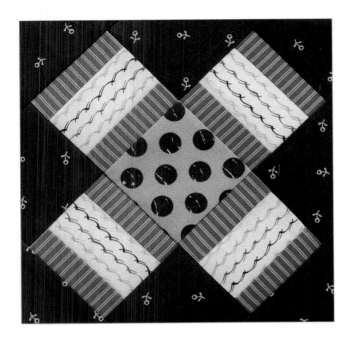

Radio Waves

• PAT SLOAN •

An email that changed my life asked, "Would you like to produce and host an Internet radio show about quilting?" Impulsively, I replied, "Sure, why not!" What I didn't know was how my love of learning people's stories would add so much richness to my life. New friendships have been formed and I'm able to share my love of quilting with a large audience, all because I said "Sure!" ~Pat

What You'll Need

A: 1 polka-dot square, 2½" × 2½"

B: 2 red print strips, 1" × 12"

C: 1 cream print strip, 1½" × 12"

1 navy print square, 8" × 8";
    cut into:

    D: 1 square, 4½" × 4½"; cut
        into quarters diagonally to
        make 4 triangles

    E: 2 squares, 3" × 3"; cut in half
        diagonally to make 4 triangles

Assembly

Press all seam allowances in the direction indicated by the arrows.

1. Sew a B strip to both long edges of the C strip to make a 2½" × 12" strip set. Cut the strip set into four 2½"-wide segments.

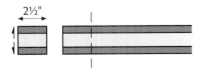

Make 1 strip set. Cut 4 segments.

2. Sew the D triangles, segments from step 1, and A square together into diagonal rows. Join the rows.

3. Fold each E triangle in half and lightly crease to mark the center of the long side. Fold the unit from step 2 in half diagonally to mark the center of each segment. Matching the center creases, sew an E triangle to each corner of the unit.

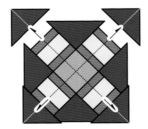

4. The block is slightly oversized. The X shape in the block center will "float" instead of touching the outer edges. Fold the block in half vertically and horizontally and slightly crease to find the center point. Place a dot on a square ruler where the 3¼" lines intersect. Align the dot on the ruler on top of the center point on the block. Trim the block to measure 6½" square.

Trim.

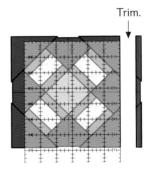

First Aid

• JANE DAVIDSON •

My family has a few favorite and well-loved quilts that we use every day; they have seen many years of wear and tear. There is no greater pleasure than mending and patching these timeless treasures—first aid for quilts. ~Jane

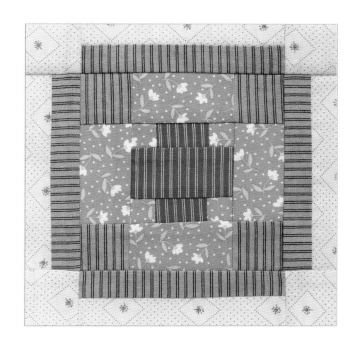

What You'll Need

1 red print square, 5" × 5"; cut into:

    A: 2 rectangles, 1" × 1½"

    B: 1 rectangle, 1½" × 2½"

1 green print square, 6" × 6"; cut into:

    C: 4 squares, 1" × 1"

    D: 4 rectangles, 1½" × 2½"

1 blue print square, 6" × 6"; cut into:

    E: 4 squares, 1½" × 1½"

    F: 4 rectangles, 1" × 4½"

1 yellow print square, 6" × 6"; cut into:

    G: 4 rectangles, 1" × 4½"

    H: 4 squares, 1½" × 1½"

Assembly

Press all seam allowances in the direction indicated by the arrows.

1. Sew C squares to the ends of an A rectangle. Make two units that measure 1" × 2½". Sew the units to the sides of the B rectangle to make a block center that measures 2½" square.

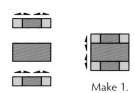

Make 1.

2. Sew E squares to the ends of a D rectangle. Make two units that measure 1½" × 4½".

Make 2.

3. Join the units from step 3, two D rectangles, and the block center. The unit should measure 4½" square.

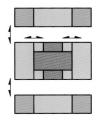

Make 1.

4. Join one F and one G rectangle along their long edges. Make four units that measure 1½" × 4½". Sew H squares to both ends of two of the units. Those units should measure 1½" × 6½".

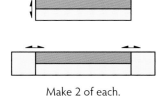

Make 2 of each.

5. Arrange and sew the units in rows as shown. Press. Join the rows to make a 6½" block. Press.

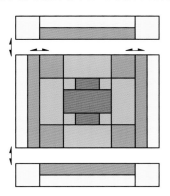

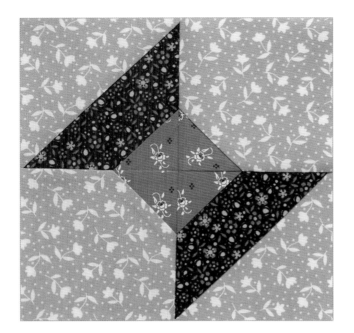

Nancy's Spool

• NANCY ZIEMAN •

The late Nancy Zieman shared, "I'm living my best quilting life when I'm spending creative time with sewing friends. This block represents the annual creative getaways with my friend Mary Mulari at her home in northern Minnesota, and also my quilting dates with my landscape quilting buddy Natalie Sewell at her home studio in Madison, Wisconsin." ~Nancy

What You'll Need

1 tan print square, 8" × 8"; cut into:

A: 1 square, 3⅞" × 3⅞"

D: 2 squares, 3½" × 3½"

B: 1 navy print square, 3⅞" × 3⅞"

C: 4 red print squares, 1¾" × 1¾"

Optional: Use your favorite half-square-triangle tool, such as a No-Hassle Triangles Gauge.

Assembly

Press all seam allowances in the direction indicated by the arrows.

1. Draw a diagonal line from corner to corner on the wrong side of the A and C squares.

2. Referring to "Triangle Squares" on page 137, place the A square on the B square with right sides together. Sew, cut, and press to make two half-square-triangle units. The units should measure 3½" square.

Make 2.

3. Referring to "Stitch and Flip" on page 137, place a C square on the B corner of a half-square-triangle unit. Sew, trim, and press. Make two.

Make 2.

4. Referring to "Stitch and Flip," place a C square on one corner of a D square. Sew, trim, and press. Make two.

Make 2.

5. Arrange and sew the pieced units in rows as shown. Press. Sew the rows together to make a 6½" block. Press.

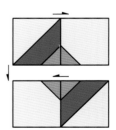

Double Dutch

• KAREN COSTELLO SOLTYS •

I'm originally from the land of the Pennsylvania Dutch, home to one of my favorite treats, shoofly pie. So it was a natural that the Shoofly block became near and dear to me. Here I've paired it with another classic block, the humble Nine Patch, and repeated both motifs for double the fun! ~Karen

What You'll Need

A: 10 blue print squares, 1½" × 1½"

B: 10 red print squares, 1½" × 1½"

C: 24 yellow print squares, 1½" × 1½"

Assembly

Press all seam allowances in the direction indicated by the arrows.

1. To make the nine-patch units, arrange five A squares and four C squares in three rows. Sew the squares together into rows and press. Join the rows and press. Make two units that measure 3½" square.

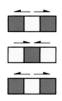

Make 2.

2. Layer a C square right sides together with a B square. Sew diagonally from corner to corner. (You can mark the diagonal line if you wish, but it's a short distance and you may want to eyeball it.) Press and trim the excess corner fabric, leaving a ¼" seam allowance. Make eight half-square-triangle units, 1½" square.

Make 8.

3. To make the shoofly units, arrange four half-square-triangle units, four C squares, and one B square in three rows. Sew the units and squares together into rows and press. Join the rows and press. Make two units that measure 3½" square.

Make 2.

4. Lay out the two nine-patch and two shoofly units in two rows as shown. Sew the units into rows and press. Join the rows and press to make a 6½" block.

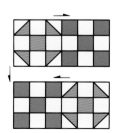

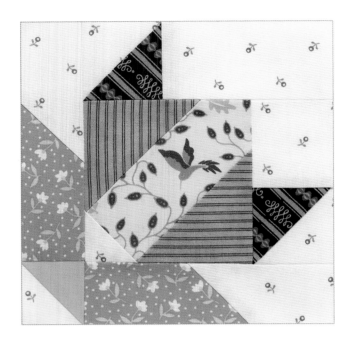

Tulip in Bloom

• NADRA RIDGEWAY •

I've recently discovered gardening and really love it. It's as joyful and relaxing as quilting and the beautiful blooms are a delightful reward, just like a finished quilt. When I'm not in my studio, you'll find me working in the flowerbeds in the courtyard of our little farm. Tulip in Bloom is inspired by the beautiful sight of my first tulips this spring. ~Nadra

What You'll Need

A: 1 navy print square, 3" × 3"

B: 2 medium blue print squares, 2¾" × 2¾"

C: 1 light blue floral square, 3¾" × 3¾"

D: 2 dark green print rectangles, 1¾" × 3¾"

E: 1 light green solid square, 2½" × 2½"

1 cream print square, 10" × 10"; cut into:

    F: 1 square, 1½" × 1½"

    G: 1 rectangle, 2" × 2¼"

    H: 2 rectangles, 1¾" × 3¼"

    I: 1 rectangle, 2" × 3¾"

    J: 1 square, 2½" × 2½"

    K: 1 square, 3" × 3"

Assembly

Press all seam allowances in the direction indicated by the arrows.

1. Draw a diagonal line from corner to corner on the wrong side of the K square. Referring to "Triangle Squares" on page 137, place the K square on the A square with right sides together. Sew, cut, and press to make two half-square-triangle units. Trim the units to measure 2" square.

Make 2.

2. Sew the G rectangle to one half-square-triangle unit to make a unit that measures 2" × 3¾". Sew the I rectangle to the remaining half-square-triangle unit to make a unit that measures 2" × 5¼". Be sure to orient the half-square-triangle units as shown.

Make 1 of each.

3. Draw a diagonal line from corner to corner on the wrong side of the B and F squares.

4. Referring to "Stitch and Flip" on page 137, place a B square on one corner of the C square. Sew, trim, and press. Place a B square on the opposite corner of the C square. Sew, trim, and press. Place the F square on the lower-left corner of the C square as shown. Sew, trim, and press to complete the block center.

Make 1.

5. Join the units from step 2 and the block center as shown. The tulip unit should measure 5¼" square.

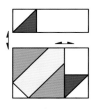

Make 1.

6. Draw a diagonal line from corner to corner on the wrong side of the J square. Referring to "Triangle Squares," place the J square on the E square with right sides together. Sew, cut, and press to make two half-square-triangle units. Trim the units to measure 1¾" square. Discard or set aside one unit for another project.

Make 1.

7. On the wrong side of one H rectangle, measure 1¾" from the lower-left corner and mark a dot. Draw a line from the dot to the lower-right corner. Place the H rectangle on a D rectangle, right sides together. Using the stitch-and-flip method, sew, trim, and press. The leaf unit should measure 1¾" × 5¼".

Make 1.

8. On the wrong side of the remaining H rectangle, measure up 1¾" from the lower-right corner and mark a dot. Draw a line from the dot to the lower-left corner. Place the H rectangle on a D rectangle, right sides together. Sew, trim, and press. The reversed leaf unit should measure 1¾" × 5¼".

Make 1 unit.

9. Arrange and sew the pieced units in rows as shown. Press. Sew the rows together to make a 6½" block. Press.

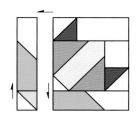

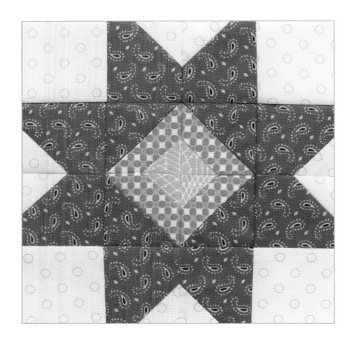

Point Taken

• SUSAN ACHE •

Who says a star has to have points? With this fun star, you don't have to worry about chopping off the points—that's part of the design! Point Taken is a perfect example of how using specific pressing directions can nest the seams and make sewing easier. ~Susan

What You'll Need

A: 2 green print squares, 2⅜" × 2⅜"; cut in half diagonally to make 4 triangles

1 red print square, 9" × 9"; cut into:

 B: 2 squares, 2⅜" × 2⅜"; cut in half diagonally to make 4 triangles

 C: 8 squares, 2" × 2"

D: 4 yellow print squares, 1¼" × 1¼"

1 cream print square, 7" × 7"; cut into:

 E: 8 squares, 1¼" × 1¼"

 F: 4 squares, 2" × 2"

Assembly

Press all seam allowances in the direction indicated by the arrows.

1. Sew an A triangle to a B triangle to make a half-square-triangle unit. Make four units that measure 2" square. Draw a diagonal line from corner to corner on the wrong side of the D squares. Referring to "Stitch and Flip" on page 137, place a D square on the A corner of a half-square-triangle unit. Sew, trim, and press. Make four.

Make 2 of each.

2. Arrange and sew the units in rows, rotating them as shown at right. Press. Sew the rows together to make the block center that measures 3½" square.

3. Draw a diagonal line from corner to corner on the wrong side of the E squares. Using the stitch-and-flip method, sew an E square on one corner of a C square. Make eight and press. Join two units, nesting the seams as shown, to make a side unit. Make four side units that measure 2" × 3½".

Make 4 of each.   Make 4.

4. Sew the F squares, four side units, and the block center together in three rows as shown. Press. Join the rows and press to make a 6½" block.

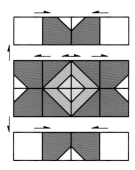

There's Always One

• JENNIFER KELTNER •

No matter how many times I put a block together, or how careful I am to place them next to my machine before sewing, in the end it seems like there's always one element that's turned the wrong direction. Much like in real life when my ducks appear to be all lined up, there's always one more idea, final thought, or last chance. ~Jennifer

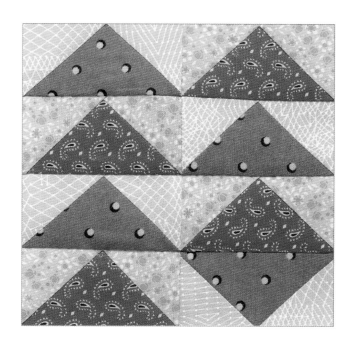

What You'll Need

A: 8 yellow print squares, 2" × 2"
B: 8 yellow check squares, 2" × 2"
C: 4 red print rectangles, 2" × 3½"
D: 4 red dot rectangles, 2" × 3½"

Assembly

Press all seam allowances in the direction indicated by the arrows.

1. Draw a diagonal line from corner to corner on the wrong side of the A and B squares.

2. Referring to "Stitch and Flip" on page 137, place an A square on one end of a C rectangle, right sides together. Sew, trim, and press. Repeat on the opposite corner and press to make a flying-geese unit that measures 2" × 3½". Make four units.

Make 4.

3. Repeat step 2 using the B squares and D rectangles to make four flying-geese units.

Make 4.

4. Arrange the eight flying-geese units as shown, alternating the fabrics and rotating one unit to point down. Sew the units into columns and press. Join the columns and press to make a 6½" block.

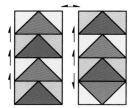

TRY IT! YOU MIGHT LIKE IT!

I'm not one for sewing with too many gadgets. But after sewing alongside some of the best quilt designers I know, I noticed one gadget that kept appearing on their cutting mats: Bloc-Loc Flying Geese rulers. Cutting is my least favorite part of the quilting process; sewing oversized blocks and trimming them down isn't a technique I'm drawn to. But, I gave it a try, and guess what? The Bloc-Loc Flying Geese ruler gave me a perfectly shaped unit every time. So, if your flying geese aren't all you want them to be, try a specialty ruler like Bloc-Loc. You might just like it!

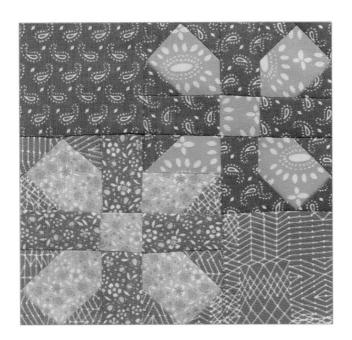

In the Hoop

• JANE DAVIDSON •

As an 8-year-old at school, I was taught to make a small tablecloth using gingham and a large cross stitch. This was my introduction to embroidery, which I've loved ever since. Now I collect antique tablecloths and doilies, cherishing the work of their unknown crafters and wondering what their lives were like as they placed their work in a hoop and stitched. ~Jane

What You'll Need

1 blue print piece, 7" × 10"; cut into:

    A: 10 squares, 1¼" × 1¼"

    B: 4 rectangles, 1¼" × 2"

    C: 1 square, 2¾" × 2¾"

1 green print square, 7" × 7"; cut into:

    D: 3 squares, 2" × 2"

    E: 1 rectangle, 1¼" × 2"

    F: 1 square, 1¼" × 1¼"

1 red print #1 piece, 7" × 10"; cut into:

    G: 10 squares, 1¼" × 1¼"

    H: 1 square, 2¾" × 2¾"

1 red print #2 piece, 3" × 6"; cut into:

    I: 4 rectangles, 1¼" × 2"

1 yellow print square, 7" × 7"; cut into:

    J: 3 squares, 2" × 2"

    K: 1 rectangle, 1¼" × 2"

    L: 1 square, 1¼" × 1¼"

Assembly

Press all seam allowances in the direction indicated by the arrows.

1. Draw a diagonal line from corner to corner on the wrong sides of the A and G squares.

2. Referring to "Stitch and Flip" on page 137, sew three A squares on each D square as shown. Make three units that measure 2" square. Repeat to make three units using the G and J squares.

Make 3 of each.

3. Sew the remaining A square on one end of the E rectangle. Sew the remaining G square on one end of the K rectangle.

Make 1 of each.

4. Sew the F square between two B rectangles. Sew the L square between two I rectangles. Both units should measure 1¼" × 4¼".

Make 1 of each.

5. Lay out the units, the two remaining B rectangles, the two remaining I rectangles, the C square, and the H square as shown. Join the pieces into rows and press. Join the rows and press to make a 6½" block.

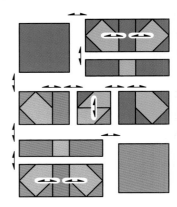

Summer Reading

• HEATHER GIVANS •

I love reading in the summer, whether it's reading from a physical book or listening to audiobooks while sewing. Often you can find my whole family lined up on our front porch, reading books on a Sunday afternoon. I can imagine no better vacation then one that involves reading for hours on end. Delightful! ~Heather

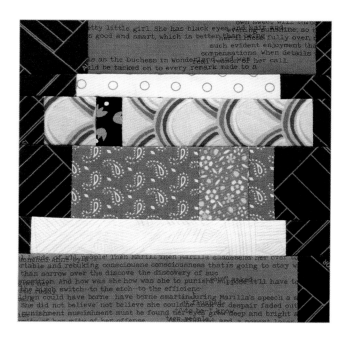

What You'll Need

1 navy tone-on-tone square, 6" × 6"; cut into:

- **A:** 3 rectangles, 1½" × 2"
- **B:** 3 rectangles, 1" × 1½"
- **C:** 2 rectangles, ¾" × 1½"
- **D:** 1 square, 1¼" × 1¼"
- **E:** 1 rectangle, ¾" × 1¼"
- **F:** 1 rectangle, 1" × 1¾"

G: 1 royal blue print rectangle, 1½" × 4¾"

H: 1 cream print rectangle, 1" × 4½"

1 light blue piece, 2" × 6"; cut into:

- **I:** 1 square, 1½" × 1½"
- **J:** 1 rectangle, 1½" × 4¼"

K: 1 navy floral rectangle, 1" × 1½"

1 blue paisley square, 4" × 4"; cut into:

- **L:** 1 rectangle, 2" × 3"
- **M:** 1 rectangle, 1" × 2"

N: 1 red print rectangle, 1½" × 2"

O: 1 light blue tone-on-tone rectangle, 1¼" × 5½"

P: 1 medium blue print rectangle, 1¾" × 6"

Assembly

Press all seam allowances in the direction indicated by the arrows.

1. Arrange the A–P pieces in six rows as shown. Sew the pieces into rows and press.

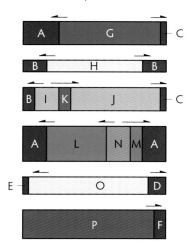

2. Sew the rows together and press to make a 6½" block.

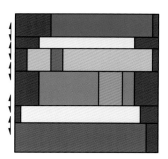

Sparkling Star

• LINDA NITZEN •

I live in the suburbs and rarely see many stars in the sky because of nighttime light pollution. As a family, we enjoy dirt-bike riding in the desert. There, before the moon rises, the sky sparkles with the light of thousands of stars. It's a beautiful time to reflect upon the day's events and dream of tomorrow's adventures. ~Linda

What You'll Need

1 navy tone-on-tone square,
  10" × 10"; cut into:

  A: 16 squares, 1½" × 1½"

  B: 4 rectangles, 1¾" × 2¾"

  C: 2 squares, 2" × 2"

1 yellow print #1 square, 8" × 8";
  cut into:

  D: 2 squares, 1½" × 1½"

  E: 4 rectangles, 1¾" × 2¾"

  F: 2 squares, 2" × 2"

1 yellow print #2 square, 6" × 6";
  cut into:

  G: 2 squares, 1½" × 1½"

  H: 4 squares, 2" × 2"

Template plastic

Assembly

Press all seam allowances in the direction indicated by the arrows.

1. Arrange three A squares and one D square in two rows as shown. Sew the units into rows and press. Join the rows and press. Make two corner units that measure 2½" square.

Make 2.

2. Repeat step 1 using three A squares and one G square to make two corner units.

Make 2.

3. Draw a diagonal line from corner to corner on the wrong side of the H squares. Referring to "Triangle Squares" on page 137, place an H square on a C square with right sides together. Sew, cut, and press to make two half-square-triangle units. Make four units and trim them to measure 1½" square.

Make 4.

4. Make a template using template plastic and the triangle pattern on page 17. Trace the template onto the wrong side of each of the B and E rectangles. Cut out along the marked lines.

5. Join one B and one E triangle, slightly offsetting the triangles as shown. Make four units that measure 1½" × 2½".

⅛"

Make 4.

6. Sew an A square to a half-square-triangle unit and press. Sew the unit to a unit from step 5 as shown and press. Make four side units that measure 2½" square.

Make 4.

7. Using the leftover H squares, place an H square on an F square with right sides together. Sew, cut, and press to make two half-square-triangle units. Make four units and trim them to measure 1½" square.

Make 4.

8. Join the units from step 7 to make the block center. Press. It should measure 2½" square.

Make 1.

9. Arrange the four corner units, four side units, and the block center in three rows as shown. Sew the units into rows and press. Join the rows and press to make a 6½" block.

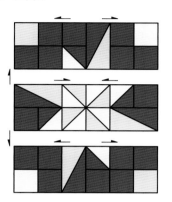

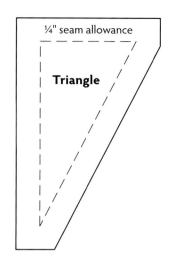

¼" seam allowance

Triangle

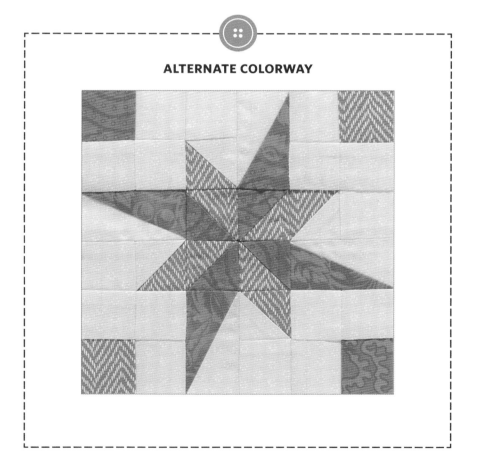

ALTERNATE COLORWAY

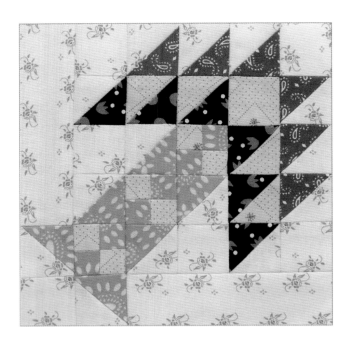

Out on a Limb

• CARRIE NELSON •

While I wasn't a particularly agile kid, I did like climbing trees. I also liked crawling out on tree limbs as far as I could for a better view. That attitude is also how I like to quilt—take a chance. While the branch might break, the experience and the view are probably worth the risk. The good news is that with quilting, you aren't likely to break any bones. ~Carrie

What You'll Need

1 cream print piece, 8" × 10"; cut into:

    A: 7 squares, 2" × 2"

    B: 6 squares, 1½" × 1½"

    C: 2 rectangles, 1½" × 4½"

1 yellow print piece, 4" × 8"; cut into:

    D: 2 squares, 2" × 2"

    E: 1 strip, 1" × 7"

    F: 1 square, 1½" × 1½"

G: 3 blue print squares, 2" × 2"

H: 3 navy print squares, 2" × 2"

1 green print piece, 4" × 8"; cut into:

    I: 3 squares, 2" × 2"

    J: 1 strip, 1" × 7"

Assembly

Press all seam allowances in the direction indicated by the arrows.

1. Draw a diagonal line from corner to corner on the wrong side of the A and D squares.

2. Referring to "Triangle Squares" on page 137, layer three A squares with the G squares, right sides together. Sew, cut, and press to make six half-square-triangle units. Trim the units to 1½" square. Repeat to make two A/H units and six A/I units.

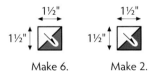

Make 6.   Make 2.

Make 6.

3. Repeat step 2 using the D squares and remaining H squares to make four half-square-triangle units that measure 1½" square.

Make 4.

4. Sew the J strip to the E strip to make a strip set that measures 1½" × 7". Cut the strip set into six 1"-wide segments.

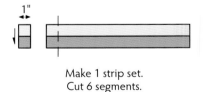

Make 1 strip set.
Cut 6 segments.

5. Sew two segments together as shown to make a four-patch unit. Make three units that measure 1½" square.

Make 3.

6. Arrange and sew the half-square-triangle units, four-patch units, five B squares, and the F square in five rows as shown. Sew the units into rows and press. Join the rows and press. The unit should measure 5½" square.

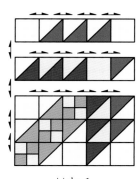

Make 1.

7. Join a C rectangle to a half-square-triangle unit, noting the direction of the diagonal seamline; press. Sew the strip to the left side of the unit from step 6 and press. Join the remaining B square, half-square-triangle unit, and C rectangle as shown; press. Sew the strip to the bottom of the block and press to make a 6½" block.

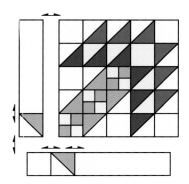

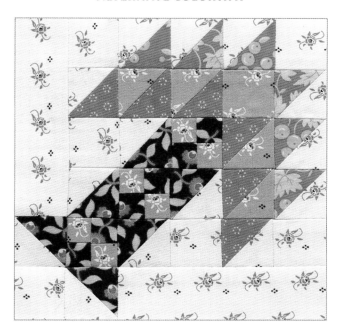

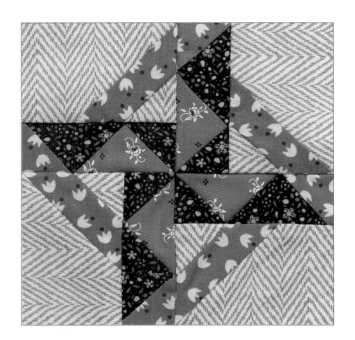

Pinwheel Magic

• MARILYN FOREMAN •

Playing with fabric and dreaming up new designs are my favorite parts of quilting. My mind starts spinning with all the possibilities. What happens if I use this color vs. that color, or if I switch around the block pieces? It's like magic, seeing how each little tweak changes the quilt, and it's so satisfying to discover your favorite color combinations! ~Marilyn

What You'll Need

1 tan print square, 8" × 8";
   cut into:
   A: 4 rectangles, 2½" × 3½"
   B: 4 squares, 1½" × 1½"
1 blue print piece, 8" × 6"; cut into:
   C: 4 squares, 2½" × 2½"
   D: 2 squares, 2" × 2"
E: 4 red print rectangles,
   1½" × 2½"
1 navy print piece, 6" × 7"; cut into:
   F: 8 squares, 1½" × 1½"
   G: 2 squares, 2" × 2"

Assembly

Press all seam allowances in the direction indicated by the arrows.

1. Draw a diagonal line from corner to corner on the wrong side of the B, C, D, and F squares.

2. Referring to "Stitch and Flip" on page 137, place a C square on the left end of an A rectangle. Sew, trim, and press. Make four.

Make 4.

3. Using the stitch-and-flip method, place a B square on the C corner of each unit. Sew, trim, and press. Make four.

Make 4.

4. Using the stitch-and-flip method, sew two marked F squares to each E rectangle to make four flying-geese units.

Make 4.

5. Referring to "Triangle Squares" on page 137, place a marked D square right sides together with each G square. Sew, cut, and press to make four half-square-triangle units. Trim the units to 1½" square.

Make 4.

6. Sew a half-square-triangle unit to a flying-geese unit as shown and press. Make four units that measure 1½" × 3½".

Make 4.

7. Sew a unit from step 3 to each unit from step 6 to make four units that measure 3½" square. Press.

Make 4.

8. Arrange the four pieced units in two rows, rotating them as shown. Sew the units into rows and press. Join the rows and press to make a 6½" block.

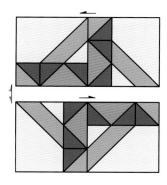

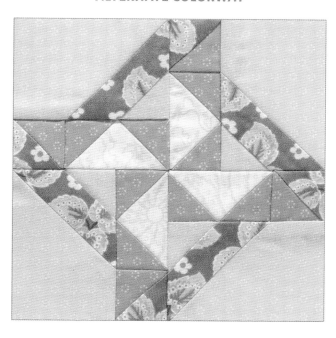

Grandma's Abiding Faith

• JILL SHAULIS •

One of my fondest childhood memories is of my Grandma singing and playing her pump organ. I can still hear her playing hymns like The Old Rugged Cross, *which is why I created a version of the Cross and Crown block. ~Jill*

What You'll Need

1 cream print square, 8" × 8"; cut into:

A: 2 squares, 2¾" × 2¾"
B: 4 squares, 1¾" × 1¾"
C: 4 rectangles, 1½" × 3"

1 navy print square, 8" × 8"; cut into:

D: 4 squares, 2¾" × 2¾"
E: 1 square, 1½" × 1½"

F: 2 red print squares, 2¾" × 2¾"
G: 4 green print squares, 1¾" × 1¾"

Assembly

Press all seam allowances in the direction indicated by the arrows.

1. Referring to "Triangle Squares" on page 137, draw a diagonal line from corner to corner on the wrong side of the A and F squares.

2. Place a marked A square on a D square with right sides together.

Sew, cut, and press. Repeat to make a total of four half-square-triangle units. Sew the marked F squares to the remaining D squares to make four half-square-triangle units.

Make 4.

Make 4.

3. Pair two different half-square-triangle units and place them right sides together, aligning the seams. Draw a diagonal line from corner to corner on the wrong side of the top unit, perpendicular to the seams. Sew ¼" from both sides of the line; cut and press to make two hourglass units. Make eight units and trim them to 1¾" square.

1¾"
1¾"
Make 8.

4. Arrange and sew one B square, two hourglass units, and one G square in two rows as shown. Press. Sew the rows together and press. The unit should measure 3" square. Repeat to make a total of four units.

Make 4.

5. Sew the four pieced units, the C rectangles, and the E square into three rows as shown. Press. Join the rows and press to make a 6½" block.

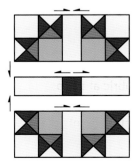

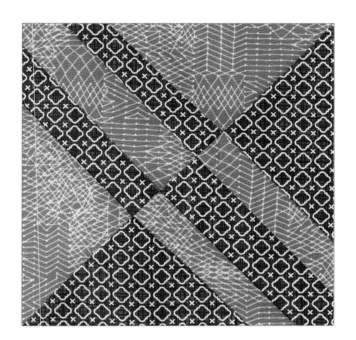

Match Point

• MARY HONAKER •

When you're editing video clips together, you look for a place where two different videos can join in a way that appears to be one cohesive story. This block gives two fabrics a chance to tell one story, while maintaining their own identity . . . with a few great match points! ~Mary

What You'll Need

A: 1 red print square, 9½" × 9½"; cut in half diagonally to make 2 triangles (1 will be extra)

B: 1 blue print square, 9½" × 9½"; cut in half diagonally to make 2 triangles (1 will be extra)

Assembly

Press all seam allowances in the direction indicated by the arrows.

1. Sew the A triangle to the B triangle to make a half-square-triangle unit.

2. Orient the unit with the seam line in a horizontal position and the B fabric at the bottom. Align the 2" line on a ruler with the top and bottom points. Use a rotary cutter to cut along the edge of the ruler. Rotate the unit 180°, measure 2" from the top and bottom points, and cut along the edge of the ruler.

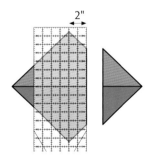

3. Align the ¾" line on a ruler with the top and bottom points. Use a rotary cutter to cut along the edge of the ruler. Rotate the unit 180°, measure ¾" from the top and bottom points, and cut along the edge of the ruler.

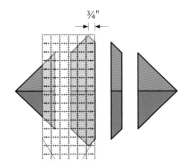

4. Rearrange the pieces so that the A and B fabrics alternate as shown.

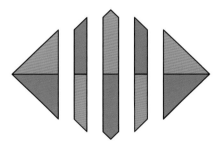

5. Sew the pieces together, making sure to match the seam intersections, and press. Trim the block to measure 6½" square.

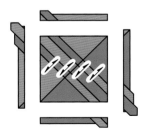

Twice as Much!

• SHRUTI DANDEKAR •

I've been a huge fan of scale ever since I was an architecture student. In this block, I play with size and scale using one of the most basic units in quilting—a half-square triangle. ~Shruti

What You'll Need

1 red print square, 8" × 8";
    cut into:
    A: 2 squares, 2" × 2"
    B: 1 square, 3" × 3"
    C: 1 square, 4" × 4"
1 navy floral square, 10" × 10";
    cut into:
    D: 3 squares, 2" × 2"
    E: 1 square, 3" × 3"
    F: 1 square, 4" × 4"
    G: 1 square, 1¼" × 1¼"
    H: 1 square, 3½" × 3½"

Assembly

Press all seam allowances in the direction indicated by the arrows.

1. Referring to "Triangle Squares" on page 137, draw a diagonal line from corner to corner on the wrong side of the A, B, and C squares.

2. Place a marked A square right sides together with a D square. Sew, cut, and press to make two half-square-triangle units. Make four units and trim them to 1¼" square. Discard or set aside one unit for another project.

Make 4.

3. Place the marked B square right sides together with the E square. Sew, cut, and press to make two half-square-triangle units. Trim the units to 2" square.

Make 2.

4. Place the marked C square right sides together with the F square. Sew, cut, and press to make two half-square-triangle units. Trim the units to 3½" square.

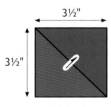

Make 2.

5. Arrange and sew three units from step 1 and the G square in two rows as shown. Press. Sew the rows together and press. The unit should measure 2" square.

Make 1.

6. Join two units from step 3, the unit from step 5, and the remaining D square as shown. Press. The unit should measure 3½" square.

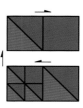

Make 1.

7. Arrange and sew the two units from step 4, the unit from step 6, and the H square in two rows as shown. Press. Sew the rows together and press to make a 6½" block.

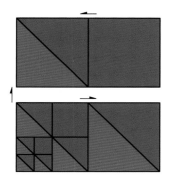

ALTERNATE COLORWAY

Cathedral Windows

• JENNY DOAN •

When I was a teenager, I learned how to stitch this block together by hand, and you know what? I still have that little baggie filled with unstitched squares because the technique was so overwhelming! But have no fear—the method below is quick and easy. I think you're going to love it! ~Jenny

What You'll Need

A: 4 cream print squares, 3½" × 3½"

B: 5 assorted print squares, 3½" × 3½"

Assembly

Press all seam allowances in the direction indicated by the arrows.

1. Fold all four A squares in half diagonally and lightly finger-press.

Make 4.

2. Pin a folded triangle on one corner of a B square. Make four.

Make 4.

3. Arrange the four units in two rows with the cream triangles in the center. Sew the units together in rows and press. Join the rows and press.

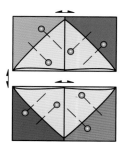

Make 1.

4. Center the remaining B square over the seams and pin in place.

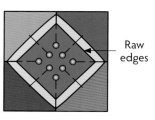

5. Turn the folded edge of the cream triangles over the raw edges of the B square. Topstitch along the folded edges and press to make a 6½" block.

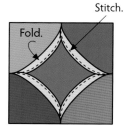

Radio Silence

• ANNE MARIE CHANY •

My first years of quilting were done during babies' nap times. I sewed in welcome silence, accompanied only by baby-monitor static. The white noise and hum of the sewing machine became therapeutic. The radio silence was synonymous with "me time" and symbolic of stress relief. ~Anne Marie

What You'll Need

1 cream print square, 10" × 10";
   cut into:
   A: 4 squares, 2¼" × 2¼"
   B: 12 squares, 1½" × 1½"

1 navy print square, 10" × 10";
   cut into:
   C: 4 squares, 2¼" × 2¼"
   D: 4 rectangles, 1½" × 2½"
   E: 4 squares, 1½" × 1½"
   F: 1 square, 2½" × 2½"

G: 4 blue print rectangles,
   1½" × 2½"

Assembly

Press all seam allowances in the direction indicated by the arrows.

1. Draw a diagonal line from corner to corner on the wrong side of the A squares and eight of the B squares.

2. Referring to "Triangle Squares" on page 137, place a marked A square right sides together with each C square. Sew, cut, and press to make eight half-square-triangle units. Trim the units to 1½" square

Make 8.

3. Referring to "Stitch and Flip" on page 137, sew two marked B squares to each D rectangle to make four flying-geese units.

Make 4.

4. Arrange the remaining B squares, G rectangles, E squares, the half-square-triangle units, the flying-geese units, and the F square in three rows as shown. Sew the units into rows and press. Join the rows to make a 6½" block. Press.

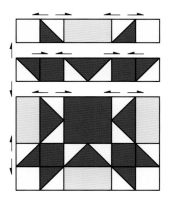

Big Sun

• LISSA ALEXANDER •

I made this block during Hurricane Harvey. So many people were affected by this storm, and I remember wishing that a Big Sun would come and dry up all the rain. To me, the best quilting life is seeing people use their gift of quilting to help others. During hard times, quilters always come together to help raise funds and make quilts for those in need. ~Lissa

What You'll Need

6 assorted cream print squares, 5" × 5"; cut into:
- **A:** 8 squares, 2" × 2"
- **C:** 16 squares, 1½" × 1½"

9 assorted print squares, 5" × 5", cut into:
- **B:** 8 rectangles, 1¼" × 3"
- **D:** 8 squares, 1½" × 1½"

1 yellow print square, 6" × 6", cut into:
- **E:** 2 rectangles, 1½" × 4½"
- **F:** 2 rectangles, 1½" × 2½"

G: 1 navy stripe square, 2½" × 2½"

Template plastic

Assembly

Press all seam allowances in the direction indicated by the arrows.

1. Make plastic templates using the A and B patterns on page 29. Trace an A template onto each of the A squares. Trace a B template onto each of the B rectangles. Cut out eight of each shape.

2. Join two A and two B shapes to make a unit that measures 1½" × 2½". Make four units.

Make 4.

3. Draw a diagonal line from corner to corner on the wrong side of 12 of the C squares.

4. Place a marked C square on each D square with right sides together. Sew on the line, press, and trim the excess corner fabric, leaving a ¼" seam allowance. Make eight half-square-triangle units.

Make 8.

5. Referring to "Stitch and Flip" on page 137, sew marked C squares on each corner of an E rectangle as shown, noting the direction of the diagonal lines. Sew, trim, and press. Make two.

Make 2.

6. Arrange and sew two half-square-triangle units and one unit from step 2 together as shown. Make four side units that measure 1½" × 4½".

Make 4.

7. Arrange the unit from step 5, the F rectangles, and the G square in three rows as shown. Sew the pieces into rows and press. Join the rows and press to make the block center, which should measure 4½" square.

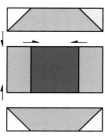

Make 1.

8. Arrange the remaining C squares, four side units, and the block center in three rows as shown. Sew the squares and units into rows and press. Join the rows and press to make a 6½" block.

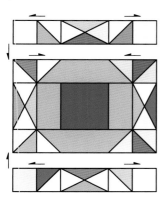

ALTERNATE COLORWAY

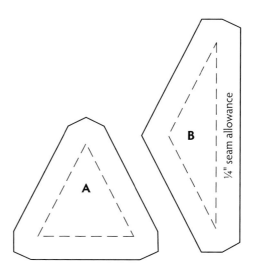

A

B

¼" seam allowance

Happy Days

• CHELSI STRATTON •

Any day filled with fabric and quilting is always the happiest of days! Quilting has become a wonderful creative outlet that always leaves my heart feeling full. There's something special about making a quilt that lasts a lifetime and will be cherished by my little ones. ~Chelsi

What You'll Need

1 light print piece, 5" × 6"; cut into:

    A: 2 squares, 1½" × 1½"

    B: 2 squares, 2½" × 2½"

1 red print piece, 4" × 6"; cut into:

    C: 2 squares, 1½" × 1½"

    D: 2 rectangles, 1½" × 2½"

E: 2 green print strips, 1½" × 4½"

F: 2 blue print strips, 1½" × 6½"

Assembly

Press all seam allowances in the direction indicated by the arrows.

1. Join A and C squares to make two units that measure 1½" × 2½".

2. Sew a D rectangle to the top of each unit. Make two units that measure 2½" square.

Make 2.

3. Arrange and sew the step 1 units and B squares together as shown to make the block center that measures 4½" square. Press.

Make 1.

4. Sew the E strips to the top and bottom of the block center. Press. Sew the F strips to opposite sides of the unit and press to make a 6½" block.

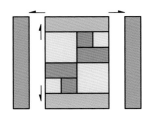

My Flock

• BRENDA RATLIFF •

Quilting is best when shared. I have the most fun sewing with my quilting guild mates and friends. I love going on weekend retreats or just hand stitching and chatting about fabrics. Quilters are wonderful people and I'm lucky to have found my flock. ~Brenda

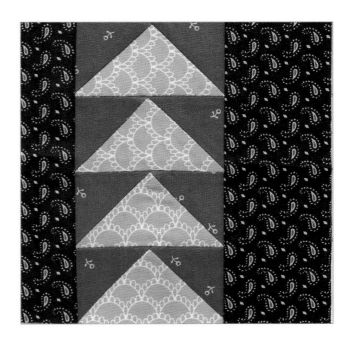

What You'll Need

A: 8 red print squares, 2" × 2"
B: 4 tan rectangles, 2" × 3½"
1 blue print piece, 5" × 7"; cut into:
    C: 1 strip, 1½" × 6½"
    D: 1 strip, 2½" × 6½"

Assembly

Press all seam allowances in the direction indicated by the arrows.

1. Draw a diagonal line from corner to corner on the wrong side of each A square.

2. Referring to "Stitch and Flip" on page 137, sew two marked A squares to each B rectangle to make four flying-geese units.

Make 4.

3. Join the flying-geese units to make a column that measures 3½" × 6½". Press.

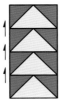

Make 1.

4. Sew the C and D strips to opposite sides of the column and press to make a 6½" block.

ACCURACY COUNTS

Small patchwork requires an accurate ¼" seam allowance. I recommend checking the units as you sew to be sure your seam allowances are consistent.

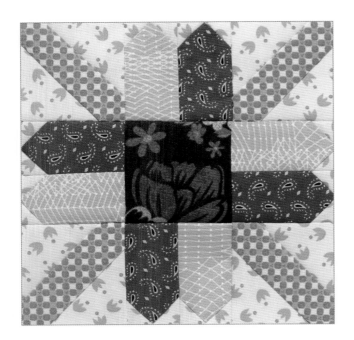

Metropolis

• SUSAN GUZMAN •

Sketching design ideas is a daily process I'm passionate about and quilting has provided me with a platform to transform many of them into patterns. My block represents fond memories I have as a young girl, when our family would visit larger cities to tour museums and historical properties. ~Susan

What You'll Need

A: 4 green print squares, 2½" × 2½"

1 cream print piece, 7" × 9"; cut into:
   B: 8 squares, 2" × 2"
   C: 16 squares, 1" × 1"

D: 4 yellow print rectangles, 1½" × 2½"

E: 4 red print rectangles, 1½" × 2½"

F: 1 navy print square, 2½" × 2½"

Assembly

Press all seam allowances in the direction indicated by the arrows.

1. Draw a diagonal line from corner to corner on the wrong side of the B and C squares.

2. Referring to "Stitch and Flip" on page 137, place a marked B square on one corner of an A square. Sew, trim, and press.

Place a marked B square on the opposite corner of the A square. Sew, cut, and press. Make four corner units that measure 2½" square.

Make 4.

3. Using the stitch-and-flip method, sew two marked C squares to each D rectangle. Sew two marked C squares to each E rectangle. Make four of each unit.

Make 4 of each.

4. Arrange and sew together one of each unit from step 3 to make a side unit. Make four side units that measure 2½" square.

Make 4.

5. Arrange the four corner units, the four side units, and the F square in three rows as shown. Sew the units and square into rows and press. Join the rows and press to make a 6½" block.

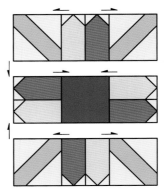

Majestic Mountains

• TARA L. BAISDEN •

I love being surrounded by beauty and peace. That beauty includes gorgeous fabrics to spark my imagination, beautiful scenery in the Appalachian Mountains where I live and work, and sparkling people with phenomenal personalities. ~Tara

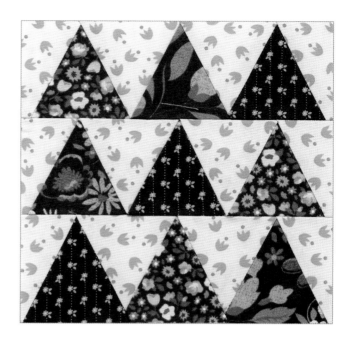

What You'll Need

3 different navy print pieces, 3" × 10"; cut into 9 squares, 3" × 3"

1 cream print square, 10" × 10"

Template plastic

Assembly

Press all seam allowances in the direction indicated by the arrows.

1. Make plastic templates using the A and B patterns. Trace the A template on each of the navy squares. Cut out each shape to make nine A triangles.

2. Trace the A templates six times on the cream square. Trace the B template three times and three times reversed on the cream square. Cut out each shape.

3. Sew the navy A triangles, cream A triangles, cream B triangles, and cream B reversed triangles into three rows as shown. Press.

Make 3.

4. Join the three triangle rows to make a 6½" block.

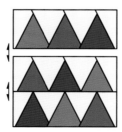

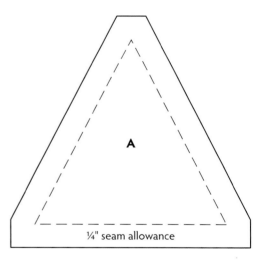

¼" seam allowance

A

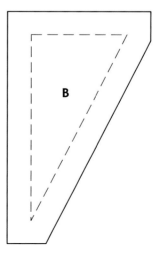

B

Antique Memories

• PAT SLOAN •

I don't come from a family of quilters. It wasn't until I met my husband's family that I even heard of quilts. When I first started quilting, I was interested in antique quilts. What was the story behind each one? Today, I often use antique quilts as inspiration. The classic Courthouse Steps is a wonderful block to use over and over again in new ways. ~Pat

What You'll Need

A: 1 tan print square, 2" × 2"

3 assorted cream print pieces, 8" × 9"; cut into:

    B: 2 strips, 1¼" × 2"

    C: 2 strips, 1¼" × 3½"

    D: 2 strips, 1¼" × 5"

3 assorted green print pieces, 8" × 9"; cut into:

    E: 2 strips, 1¼" × 3½"

    F: 2 strips, 1¼" × 5"

    G: 2 strips, 1¼" × 6½"

Assembly

Press all seam allowances in the direction indicated by the arrows.

1. Sew B strips to opposite sides of the A square and press. The unit should measure 2" × 3½".

Make 1.

2. Sew E strips to the top and bottom of the unit and press. The unit should measure 3½" square.

Make 1.

3. Continue adding strips as shown to make a 6½" block. Press each seam as a new piece is added.

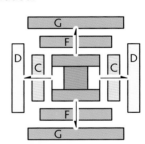

Spinning Star

• SHELLEY ROBSON •

The Spinning Star block reminds me that no matter how crazy life gets on the fringes, it can be beautiful if you pay attention to what's really important— family, friends, and happiness. If my world seems to be spinning out of control, just a little time sewing gives me back my perspective and seems to make everything better. Thank God for sewing! ~Shelley

What You'll Need

A: 4 tan check squares, 2½" × 2½"

B: 4 cream print squares, 2½" × 2½"

C: 4 navy print squares, 2½" × 2½"

D: 1 blue print square, 2½" × 2½"

E: 12 red print squares, 1½" × 1½"

Assembly

Press all seam allowances in the direction indicated by the arrows.

1. Draw a diagonal line from corner to corner on the wrong side of each C and E square.

2. Referring to "Stitch and Flip" on page 137, sew two marked E squares on opposite corners of an A square. Trim and press. Make four corner units.

Make 4.

3. Using the stitch-and-flip method, sew a marked E square to one corner of each B square to make four units.

Make 4.

4. Place a marked C square on top of a unit from step 3, right sides together so that the diagonal line bisects the red triangle. Sew on the marked line. Press. Make sure you have sewn the unit correctly, and then trim the excess corner fabric, leaving a ¼" seam allowance. Make four side units that measure 2½" square.

Make 4.

5. Arrange and sew the four corner units, four side units, and the D square in three rows as shown. Press. Join the rows to make a 6½" block.

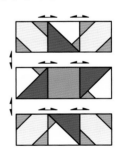

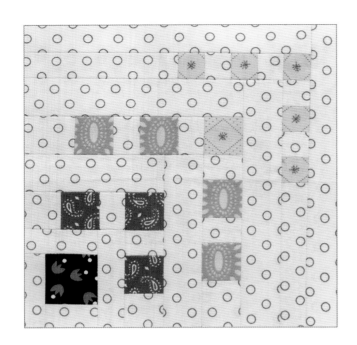

Scatter

• JESS FROST •

I've always been obsessed with tiny things. As a child (and even now!), I loved Lego. I have many favorite aspects of patchwork and quilting, and one of them is the challenge of tiny piecing. I love the focus involved in tiny piecing, which is a great escape from my busy job of raising three children. ~Jess

What You'll Need

A: 1 navy print square, 1½" × 1½"

B: 3 blue print squares, 1¼" × 1¼"

C: 4 green print squares, 1¼" × 1¼"

1 yellow print piece, 3" × 4";
   cut into:
   D: 1 square, 1¼" × 1¼"
   E: 5 squares, 1" × 1"

1 cream print square, 10" × 10";
   cut into:
   F: 1 rectangle, 1" × 1½"
   G: 2 rectangles, 1" × 2"
   H: 1 rectangle, 1" × 2½"
   I: 2 squares, 1¼" × 1¼"
   J: 6 rectangles, 1" × 1¼"
   K: 1 rectangle, 1¼" × 3¼"
   L: 1 rectangle, 1¼" × 4"
   M: 2 rectangles, 1¼" × 1½"
   N: 1 rectangle, 1¼" × 4¾"
   O: 1 rectangle, 1¼" × 5½"

P: 4 squares, 1" × 1"

Q: 2 rectangles, 1" × 3½"

R: 1 rectangle, 1" × 6"

S: 1 rectangle, 1" × 6½"

Assembly

Press all seam allowances open to reduce bulk.

1. Sew the F rectangle to the bottom of the A square and press. Sew a G rectangle to the left edge; press. Sew the remaining G rectangle to the top edge; press. Sew the H rectangle to the right edge and press. The unit should measure 2½" square.

Make 1.

2. Join an I square, a B square, and a J rectangle; press. Sew the unit to top of the unit from step 1 and press. Join two B squares, one J rectangle, and one I square; press. Sew the unit to the right edge as shown.

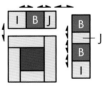

Make 1.

3. Sew the K rectangle to the top of the unit and press. Sew the L rectangle to the right edge and press. The unit should measure 4" square.

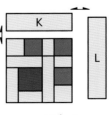

Make 1.

4. Join one M rectangle, two C squares, and two J rectangles; press. Sew the unit to the top of the unit from step 3 and press. Join the D square, two J rectangles, two C squares, and one M rectangle and press. Sew the unit to the right edge and press.

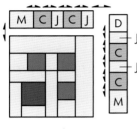

Make 1.

5. Sew the N rectangle to the top of the unit and press. Sew the O rectangle to the right edge and press. The unit should measure 5½" square.

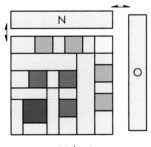

Make 1.

FUSSY-CUT MOTIFS

Sometimes it's fun to focus on one aspect of a particular print, as Jess did here. Did you notice that she fussy cut her squares to feature the same part of each print?

6. Join one Q rectangle, two E squares, and two P squares; press. Sew the unit to the top of the unit from step 5 and press. Join three E squares, two P squares, and a Q rectangle and press. Sew the unit to the right edge and press.

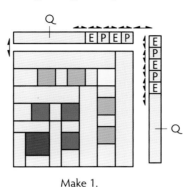

Make 1.

7. Sew the R rectangle to the top of the unit and press. Sew the S rectangle to the right edge to make a 6½" block. Press.

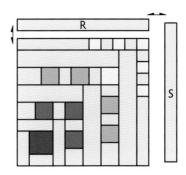

ALTERNATE COLORWAY

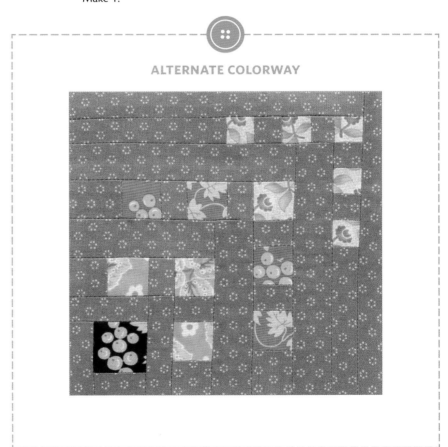

Creative Harmony

• GUDRUN ERLA •

I prefer all aspects of my life to be in balance. When the scales tilt too much one way, my creativity gets disturbed, and my joy for creating and sewing lessens. When I spend an equal amount of time taking care of myself, taking care of my family, taking care of business, and doing what I love, all the stars align and I'm a happy girl. ~Gudrun

What You'll Need

1 gray print square, 10" × 10"; cut into:

- A: 2 squares, 4" × 4"; cut in half diagonally to make 4 triangles
- B: 2 rectangles, 1¼" × 2¾"
- C: 2 squares, 2½" × 2½"
- D: 2 rectangles, 1¼" × 2"

E: 1 red print strip, 1½" × 9"

F: 1 navy print square, 2" × 2"

G: 1 blue print square, 2" × 2"

Assembly

Press all seam allowances in the direction indicated by the arrows.

1. Sew a D rectangle to the top of the F square and press. Sew a B rectangle to the right side of the unit and press. Repeat to sew a D and then a B rectangle to the G square.

Make 1 of each.

2. Sew an A triangle to the left side of each unit. Press and trim the triangles as shown.

Trim.

Make 1 of each.

3. Sew an A triangle to the bottom of each unit from step 2 and press. Make one of each.

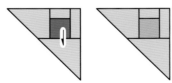

Make 1 of each.

4. Center and sew the E strip between the units as shown and press.

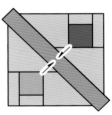

Make 1.

5. Draw a diagonal line from corner to corner on the wrong side of the C squares. Referring to "Stitch and Flip" on page 137, place the C squares on opposite corners of the block as shown. Sew, trim, and press. Square up the block to measure 6½" square.

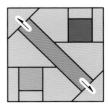

Coastline Sponge Cake

• KATARINA ROCCELLA •

Strip piecing always reminds me of baking a cake, with layers of yummy ingredients (here fabrics) placed together. The shades of these fabrics are the colors of the coastline and the sea, recalling my best childhood memories of vacations spent by the seaside, eating my favorite sponge cake. ~Katarina

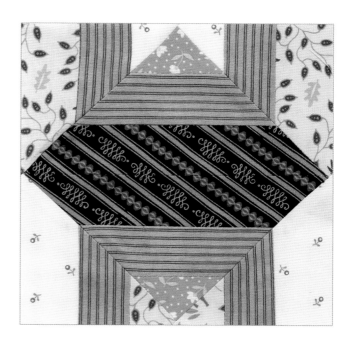

What You'll Need

A: 1 green print strip, 1½" × 15½"

1 blue stripe piece, 4" × 16";
   cut into:
      B: 1 strip, 1½" × 15½"*
      C: 1 strip, 1½" × 8½"*

D: 1 navy print strip, 1½" × 15½"

E: 1 blue floral strip, 1¾" × 8½"

F: 1 cream print strip, 1¾" × 8½"

To achieve a mitered look, cut strips along the same line of the stripe.

Assembly

Press all seam allowances in the direction indicated by the arrows.

1. Sew the A, B, and D strips together to make a strip set. Press. Cut the strip set into two 3½" × 7½" segments.

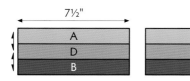

Make 1 strip set. Cut 2 segments.

2. Sew the segments together along the D strip to make a 6½" × 7½" rectangle. Place a square ruler on the rectangle, aligning the 45° line on the ruler with the center seam. Cut along two sides of the ruler. Rotate the rectangle 180°, again aligning the 45° line on the ruler with the center seam, and place the 4¾" lines on the ruler on the newly cut edges. Cut along two sides of the ruler.

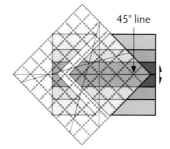

45° line

Make 1.

3. Sew the C strip between the E and F strips. Press. Cut the strip set into two 4" squares.

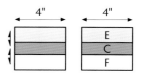

Make 1 strip set. Cut 2 segments.

4. Cut the squares in half diagonally to yield four triangles.

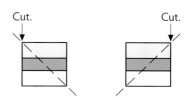

Cut.   Cut.

5. Center and sew the triangles to the center square and press. Trim the block to 6½" square.

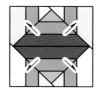

Estelle

• JOYCE BEENES •

My mom, Estelle, taught and encouraged me to sew and because of her dedication, I'm living my best quilting life. I teach classes at Thimbles quilt shop in Lockport, Illinois, and my favorite classes are beginning quilting and kids' sewing. The enthusiasm of newcomers is contagious! ~Joyce

What You'll Need

1 cream solid piece, 5" × 12"; cut into:

    A: 1 strip, 1¼" × 11"

    B: 8 squares, 1¾" × 1¾"

1 tan print piece, 4" × 12"; cut into:

    C: 1 strip, 1¼" × 11"

    D: 4 squares, 1¾" × 1¾"

1 red print piece, 5" × 8"; cut into:

    E: 8 squares, 1¾" × 1¾"

    F: 4 squares, 1¼" × 1¼"

1 navy print piece, 7" × 9"; cut into:

    G: 8 squares, 1¾" × 1¾"

    H: 8 rectangles, 1¼" × 2"

Assembly

Press all seam allowances in the direction indicated by the arrows.

1. Sew the A and C strips together to make a strip set. Press. Cut the strip set into eight 1¼"-wide segments.

Make 1 strip set. Cut 8 segments.

2. Sew two segments together as shown to make a four-patch unit. The unit should measure 2" square. Make four.

Make 4.

3. Referring to "Triangle Squares" on page 137, draw a diagonal line from corner to corner on the wrong side of the all of the B, two of the D, and four of the E squares.

4. Place a marked B square right sides together with an unmarked D square. Sew, cut, and press. Make four half-square-triangle units. Trim the units to 1¼" square.

Make 4.

5. Repeat step 4 with four marked B squares and the remaining four E squares to make eight half-square-triangle units. Use the marked E squares and four G squares to make eight half-square-triangle units.

Make 8 of each.

6. Repeat step 4 with the two remaining marked B squares and two G squares to make four half-square-triangle units. Use the marked D squares and remaining G squares to make four half-square-triangle units.

Make 4 of each.

7. Sew four B/D units together as shown to make the block center and press. The unit should measure 2" square.

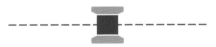

Make 1.

REDUCE BULK

Before pressing the block center and pinwheel units, use a seam ripper to remove one or two stitches from the seam allowance. Gently reposition the seam allowances to evenly distribute the fabric. Press the seam allowances in opposite directions.

---

8. Sew two B/E and two E/G units together as shown to make a corner unit and press. Make four units that measure 2" square.

Make 4.

9. Sew together two H rectangles and two B/G and two D/G units as shown to make a side unit. Make four units that measure 1¼" × 5".

Make 4.

10. Arrange the corner units, four-patch units, and the block center in three rows as shown. Sew the units into rows and press. Join the rows and press. The unit should measure 5" square.

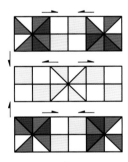

Make 1.

11. Sew a side unit to each side of the unit and press. Sew an F square to the ends of each remaining side unit and sew them to the top and bottom of the block. Press to make a 6½" block.

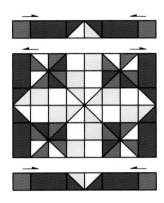

Sailor Collar

• JENNI SMITH •

I love making quilts that tell stories and evoke happy memories. I'm currently using remnants of my Grandpa Stanley's sailor collar in my patchwork. He was so inspiring—he painted landscapes on the ceilings in our house and built a caravan that turned into a boat; he had no creative boundaries! ~Jenni

What You'll Need

1 cream print square, 9" × 9"; cut into:

    A: 2 rectangles, 2¾" × 3½"

    B: 1 rectangle, 2" × 3½"

    C: 2 rectangles, 1¼" × 2¾"

    D: 6 squares, 1¼" × 1¼"

    E: 1 rectangle, 2" × 2¾"

    F: 2 squares, 1¾" × 1¾"

1 navy print piece, 7" × 8", cut into:

    G: 2 rectangles, 2¾" × 3½"

    H: 4 squares, 1¼" × 1¼"

    I: 1 rectangle, 1¼" × 2"

    J: 1 square, 1¾" × 1¾"

1 red print piece, 4" × 5", cut into:

    K: 2 rectangles, 1¼" × 2"

    L: 1 square, 1¾" × 1¾"

Template plastic

Assembly

Press all seam allowances in the direction indicated by the arrows.

1. Make a template using the pattern on page 43 and template plastic. Place two A rectangles wrong sides together. Use the template to cut out one A and one A reversed triangle. Place two G rectangles wrong sides together. Use the template to cut out one G and one G reversed triangle.

2. Sew an A triangle to a G triangle, right sides together. Sew an A reversed triangle to a G reversed triangle. The units should measure 2¾" × 3½".

Make 1 of each.

3. Referring to "Triangle Squares" on page 137, draw a diagonal line from corner to corner on the wrong side of two F squares. Layer the squares right sides together with the J and L squares. Sew, cut, and press to make two of each color combination. Trim the units to 1¼" square.

Make 2 of each.

4. Arrange and sew together three D squares, two H squares, one K rectangle, and one half-square-triangle unit from each color combination in three rows as shown. Make one of each unit. The units should measure 2¾" square.

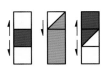

Make 1.

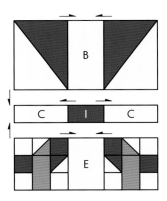

Make 1.

5. Arrange the units and the B, C, E, and I rectangles in three rows as shown. Sew the pieces into rows and press. Join the rows and press to make a 6½" block.

MIRROR IMAGES

When laying out this symmetrical block, be sure the units are mirror images of each other before sewing them together.

¼" seam allowance

Triangle

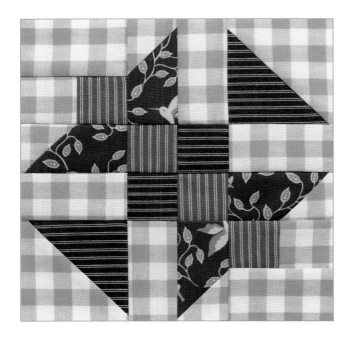

Fresh Start

• KAT WILSON TUCKER •

It's fun to start a new quilt. Exploring new ideas, fabrics, and colorways is always fresh and exciting. ~Kat

What You'll Need

1 green check square, 8" × 8"; cut into:

  A: 6 squares, 1½" × 1½"

  B: 6 rectangles, 1½" × 2½"

  C: 1 square, 2⅞" × 2⅞"; cut in half diagonally to yield 2 triangles

1 navy stripe piece, 4" × 6"; cut into:

  D: 1 square, 2⅞" × 2⅞"; cut in half diagonally to yield 2 triangles

  E: 2 squares, 1½" × 1½"

F: 4 blue print rectangles, 1½" × 2½"

G: 4 red stripe squares, 1½" × 1½"

Assembly

Press all seam allowances in the direction indicated by the arrows.

1. Referring to "Stitch and Flip" on page 137, draw a diagonal line from corner to corner on the wrong side of four A squares. Place an A square on one corner of an F rectangle, right sides together, noting the direction of the diagonal line. Sew, press, and trim. Make two of each unit.

Make 2 of each.

2. Sew A and G squares together in pairs and press. Sew a B rectangle to the bottom of each unit. Press. Make two units that measure 2½" square.

Make 2.

3. Arrange and sew one of each unit from step 1, one unit from step 2, and one G square in rows as shown. Press. Sew the rows together. Make two units that measure 3½" square.

Make 2.

4. Sew each C triangle to a D triangle to make two half-square-triangle units. Press. The units should measure 2½" square.

Make 2.

5. Arrange and sew one unit from step 4, two B rectangles, and one E square in rows as shown. Press. Sew the rows together. Make two units that measure 3½" square.

Make 2.

6. Arrange and sew the pieced units in rows as shown. Press. Sew the rows together to make a 6½" block.

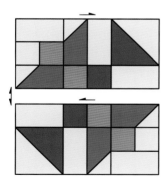

ALTERNATE COLORWAY

Balancing Reflection

• YVONNE FUCHS •

I find that quilting helps me consistently take time for myself. In those quiet moments of just me and the hum of my sewing machine, I often find myself reflecting on my life, and I like to imagine the scales of life tipping into balance. ~Yvonne

What You'll Need

1 cream print piece, 6" × 8"; cut into:

A: 2 squares, 2½" × 2½"

B: 10 squares, 1½" × 1½"

C: 2 blue print rectangles, 2½" × 4½"

D: 6 yellow print rectangles, 1½" × 2½"

1 navy print piece, 6" × 8"; cut into:

E: 2 squares, 2½" × 2½"

F: 10 squares, 1½" × 1½"

Assembly

Press all seam allowances in the direction indicated by the arrows.

1. Draw a diagonal line from corner to corner on the wrong side of the A, B, E, and F squares.

2. Referring to "Stitch and Flip" on page 137, sew two marked A squares to a C rectangle to make a flying-geese unit.

Make 1.

3. Sew two marked E squares to the remaining C rectangle to make a flying-geese unit.

Make 1.

4. Using the stitch-and-flip method, sew two marked B squares to a D rectangle to make a flying-geese unit. Make three.

Make 3.

5. Sew two marked F squares to a D rectangle to make a flying-geese unit. Make three.

Make 3.

6. Sew a B square to a unit from step 4 as shown and press. Make one of each unit.

Make 1 of each.

7. Sew an F square to a unit from step 5 as shown and press. Make one of each unit.

Make 1 of each.

8. Sew two B squares to the remaining unit from step 4; press. Sew the unit to the flying-geese unit from step 2 and press. Sew the units from step 6 to opposite sides of the unit to make the top half of the block. Press.

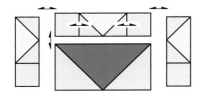

9. Sew two F squares to the remaining unit from step 5; press. Sew the unit to the flying-geese unit from step 3 and press. Sew the units from step 7 to opposite sides of the unit to make the bottom half of the block. Press.

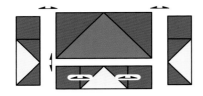

10. Sew the top and bottom halves together to make a 6½" block. Press.

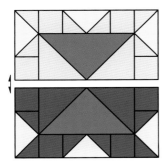

ALTERNATE COLORWAY

Star Light, Star Bright

• PAT SLOAN •

One of the amazing things about being a quilter today is our ability to talk and share with other quilters all around the world. Day and night, we're connected by the Internet. I think Star blocks also unite quilters. We've all made them, and for me, when I look up at the night sky, I see not only stars but also my quilt friends around the world. ~Pat

What You'll Need

A: 12 red print squares, 1½" × 1½"

1 cream solid square, 7" × 7";
   cut into:
   B: 8 rectangles, 1½" × 2½"
   C: 4 squares, 1½" × 1½"

D: 4 green print rectangles, 1½" × 2½"

E: 1 yellow print square, 2½" × 2½"

Assembly

Press all seam allowances in the direction indicated by the arrows.

1. Arrange and sew four A squares, the D rectangles, and the E square in three rows as shown. Press. Join the rows to make the block center and press. The unit should measure 4½" square.

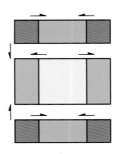

Make 1.

2. Referring to "Stitch and Flip" on page 137, draw a diagonal line from corner to corner on the wrong side of the remaining A squares. Sew two marked A squares to a B rectangle as shown. Press and trim. Make four flying-geese units.

Make 4.

3. Sew two C squares to a flying-geese unit as shown and press. Sew two B rectangles to a flying-geese unit as shown and press. Make two of each unit.

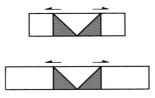

Make 2 of each unit.

4. Arrange and sew the pieced units as shown. Press. Sew the rows together to make a 6½" block.

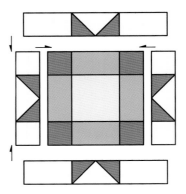

Piece in Chaos

• BETSY CHUTCHIAN •

My love of quilting centers around my love of fabric. Even with deadlines surrounding me, I adore the excitement of starting a new project by sorting through my stash for the perfect colors and prints. ~Betsy

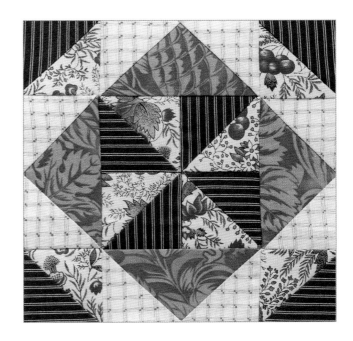

What You'll Need

A: 4 cream floral squares, 2½" × 2½"

B: 4 cream plaid squares, 2½" × 2½"; cut in half diagonally to make 8 triangles

C: 4 navy stripe squares, 2½" × 2½"

D: 1 tan print square, 4⅜" × 4⅜"; cut into quarters diagonally to make 4 triangles

Assembly

Press all seam allowances in the direction indicated by the arrows.

1. Draw a diagonal line from corner to corner on the wrong side of the A squares.

2. Referring to "Triangle Squares" on page 137, place an A square on a C square with right sides together. Sew, cut, and press to make two half-square-triangle units. Make eight units and trim them to 2" square.

Make 8.

3. Sew four units together as shown to make the block center and press.

Make 1.

4. Sew two B triangles to each D triangle as shown to make four flying-geese units. Trim the units to measure 2" × 3½".

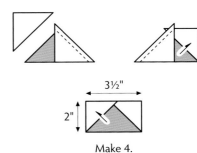

Make 4.

5. Arrange and sew the pieced units in rows as shown. Press. Sew the rows together to make a 6½" block.

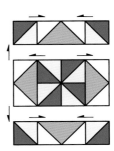

Open Arms

• MONIQUE DILLARD •

When I look at this block and the orientation of the triangles, it reminds me of open arms. My pattern-company logo depicts an open gate and an Old English sheepdog welcoming you. Although a dog can't welcome you with open arms, she sure can welcome you, and this is how I feel about my fellow quilters . . . I welcome you with open arms! ~Monique

What You'll Need

1 blue print piece, 7" × 9"; cut into:

    A: 4 squares, 1½" × 1½"

    B: 8 rectangles, 1¾" × 2½"

C: 1 cream print piece, 6" × 8"; cut into 8 rectangles, 1¾" × 2½"

D: 4 tan print squares, 1½" × 1½"

1 red stripe piece, 5" × 7"; cut into:

    E: 4 squares, 1½" × 1½"

    F: 4 rectangles, 1½" × 2½"

Assembly

Press all seam allowances in the direction indicated by the arrows.

1. Make a template using the pattern on pattern sheet 1 and template plastic. Place two B rectangles wrong sides together. Use the template to cut out one B and one B reversed triangle. Repeat to cut a total of four B and four B reversed triangles.

2. Place two C rectangles wrong sides together. Use the template to cut out one C and one C reversed triangle. Cut a total of four C and four C reversed triangles.

3. Sew a B triangle to a C triangle, right sides together. Sew a B reversed triangle to a C reversed triangle. The units should measure 1½" × 2½". Make four of each.

Make 4 of each.

4. Sew a D square to an E square. Press. Sew an F rectangle to the bottom of each unit. Repeat to make a total of four units that measure 2½" square. Press.

Make 4.

5. Sew together one unit and one unit reversed from step 3, one unit from step 4, and one A square as shown. Press. Make four units that measure 3½" square.

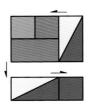

Make 4.

6. Sew the pieced units into rows as shown. Press. Sew the rows together to make a 6½" block.

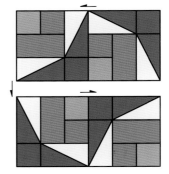

Lauren's Flower Basket

· ANNETTE PLOG ·

I adore piecing blocks and making quilts for people I love. The first quilt I made for my daughter, Lauren, used a Flower Basket block. Whenever I see this block, I think of my sweet daughter. ~Annette

What You'll Need

1 tan print square, 10" × 10"; cut into:

   A: 1 square, 4½" × 4½"

   B: 4 squares, 2½" × 2½"

   C: 2 rectangles, 2" × 3½"

1 navy print piece, 6" × 8"; cut into:

   D: 1 square, 4½" × 4½"

   E: 1 square, 2½" × 2½"

F: 1 red print square, 2½" × 2½"

G: 1 green print square, 2½" × 2½"

H: 1 blue print square, 2½" × 2½"

Assembly

Press all seam allowances in the direction indicated by the arrows.

1. Draw a diagonal line from corner to corner on the wrong side of the A and B squares.

2. Referring to "Triangle Squares" on page 137, place the A square on the D square with right sides together. Sew, cut, and press to make two half-square-triangle units. Trim the units to measure 3½" square. Discard or set one unit aside for another project.

Make 2.

3. Place a B square on the E square with right sides together. Sew, cut, and press to make two half-square-triangle units. Trim the units to measure 2" square. Repeat to make two B/F units, two B/G units, and two B/H units.

Make 2 of each.

4. Arrange six half-square-triangle units from step 3 in two rows as shown. Sew the units into rows and press. Join the rows and press. Add a C rectangle to make the top section, which should measure 3½" × 6½".

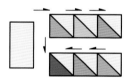

Make 1.

5. Join two half-square-triangle units from step 3 as shown. Sew a C rectangle to the bottom of the unit. Add the half-square-triangle unit from step 1 to make the bottom section, which should measure 3½" × 6½". Press.

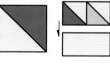

Make 1.

6. Join the top and bottom sections to make a 6½" block.

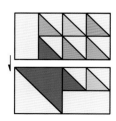

Come Together

• LEE CHAPPELL MONROE •

Sometimes stitching seems like a solitary event, but you can combat that feeling by joining a group. A few years ago, I met a new crew of stitching buddies at a retreat. We come together a few times a year in the Smoky Mountains for endless stitching, laughter, and pimento cheese. ~Lee

What You'll Need

A: 8 green print squares, 2¼" × 2¼"

1 navy print piece, 6" × 10"; cut into:

    B: 4 squares, 2¼" × 2¼"

    C: 8 squares, 1¾" × 1¾"

1 cream print piece, 5" × 12"; cut into:

    D: 4 squares, 2¼" × 2¼"

    E: 4 rectangles, 1¾" × 2¾"

1 tan check square, 8" × 8"; cut into:

    F: 8 squares, 1¾" × 1¾"

    G: 4 rectangles, 1¾" × 2¾"

H: 1 red print square, 2½" × 2½"

Assembly

Press all seam allowances in the direction indicated by the arrows.

1. Draw a diagonal line from corner to corner on the wrong side of the A, F, and C squares.

2. Referring to "Triangle Squares" on page 137, place a marked A square on each B square with right sides together. Sew, cut, and press to make eight half-square-triangle units. Place a marked A square on each D square with right sides together. Sew, cut, and press to make eight half-square-triangle units. Trim the units to measure 1½" square.

Make 8 of each.

3. Sew four units together as shown to make a corner unit. Make four units that measure 2½" square.

Make 4.

4. Referring to "Stitch and Flip" on page 137, sew two marked F squares to each E rectangle to make four flying-geese units. Sew two marked C squares to each G rectangle to make four flying-geese units. Press. Trim the units to measure 1½" × 2½".

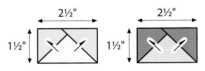

Make 4 of each.

5. Join the flying-geese units in pairs to make four side units that measure 2½" square.

Make 4.

6. Arrange the four corner units, the four side units, and the H square in three rows as shown. Sew the units into rows and press. Join the rows and press to make a 6½" block.

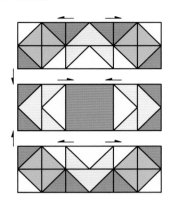

DRAWING LINES

To sew accurate half-square-triangle and flying-geese units, it's important to start with a well-marked square. Place your pen in the corner of the square and align the ruler next to it. That way the ruler is in the right spot, so the line goes to the corner and not next to it. To keep the fabric from bunching up, start in the middle and draw the line toward the corners.

ALTERNATE COLORWAY

Dutch Treat

• PAT SLOAN •

Flowers are a great inspiration for design. I love to create my own versions of flowers in a folk-art style. My style is very open and less detailed. I let the fabrics do all the work. Perhaps my love of folk art is deeply rooted in the Amish countryside, where my great-grandparents lived. The Pennsylvania Dutch influence shows itself in my simple appliqué shapes. ~Pat

What You'll Need

1 cream print square, 7" × 7", for background

1 dark print square, 2" × 2", for center dot*

1 red print square, 6" × 6", for tulips

1 green print square, 3½" × 3½", for leaves

Lightweight fusible web, 7" × 7"

Baby rickrack, 4" long, for stems

I fussy-cut the dark print so it features a red-and-pink flower in the center.

Appliqué

The appliqué patterns are on pattern sheet 1. The instructions are written for fusible appliqué. If you prefer hand appliqué, add a seam allowance as you cut the shapes. The patterns are symmetrical, so there's no need to reverse them.

1. Trace the patterns onto the fusible web, leaving ½" between the shapes. Cut out the shapes, leaving about ¼" outside the drawn lines.

2. Fuse the shapes to the wrong side of the chosen fabrics, following the manufacturer's instructions. Cut out the shapes on the drawn lines and peel away the paper backing.

3. Fold the background square in half vertically and horizontally to create creases to help with placement. Position the dot in the center, and then position the four tulips. Cut four 1"-long pieces of rickrack. For each tulip, tuck one end of the rickrack under the tulip and the other end under the dot. Add the leaves, tucking one end under the dot. Fuse in place.

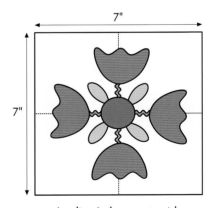

Appliqué placement guide

4. Stitch around the shapes with a machine blanket stitch to secure the edges of the appliqués. Press the block on the wrong side and trim it to 6½" square, keeping the design centered.

Fashionable Pineapple

• JANE DAVIDSON •

I love pineapples. I was very excited to see a trend of pineapples popping up everywhere recently in home wares, fabrics, and on the walkways of the Paris fashion shows. ~Jane

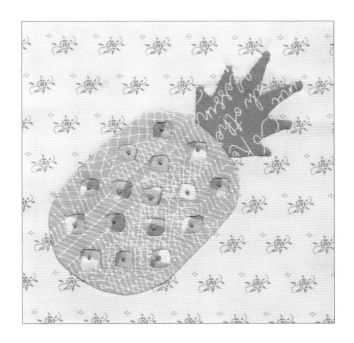

What You'll Need

1 cream print square, 7" × 7", for block background

1 green check square, 5" × 5", for pineapple background

1 yellow print square, 5" × 5", for pineapple

1 green print square, 3" × 3" for pineapple top

Template plastic or freezer paper

Pink embroidery floss

Appliqué glue

Appliqué

The appliqué patterns are on pattern sheet 1. The instructions are written for hand appliqué. Reverse the patterns for fusible appliqué.

1. Prepare the appliqués for your preferred method. Do not add a seam allowance to the pineapple background. Add a scant ¼" seam allowance around the pineapple and the pineapple top. On the pineapple, cut an X in each small square, clipping into each corner.

2. On the right side of the pineapple background, place a few drops of appliqué glue around the outer edges and position it underneath the pineapple.

3. Needle-turn appliqué (page 135) inside each square on the pineapple.

4. Position the pineapple top and pineapple on the background square and appliqué in place.

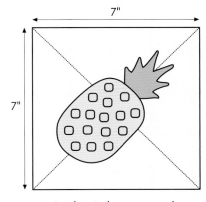

Appliqué placement guide

5. Using two strands of embroidery floss, make a French knot inside each square on the pineapple. See "Embroidery Stitches" on page 138 for stitching instructions.

6. Press the block on the wrong side and trim it to 6½" square, keeping the design centered.

Around Four Corners

• RACHAELDAISY •

I like to travel around the four corners of my imagination. Creative adventures lead me through glorious fabric gardens, under magical rainbows of color, over mountains of geometry, and through oceans of ideas. It's a place where circles can even become squares. ~Rachaeldaisy

What You'll Need

A: 1 cream print square, 3" × 3", for block center

1 navy floral piece, 9" × 11"; cut into:

> B: 2 rectangles, 2¼" × 3", for background
>
> C: 2 rectangles, 2¼" × 6½", for background
>
> D: 4 squares, 2" × 2", for circles

4 rectangles, 4" × 5", of different prints for circles; cut *each* rectangle into:

> E: 1 square, 2" × 2" (4 total)
>
> F: 1 rectangle, 2" × 3½" (4 total)

Freezer paper, 6" × 6"

Assembly and Appliqué

Press all seam allowances in the direction indicated by the arrows. The appliqué pattern is on page 57 and does not include seam allowances. The instructions are written for hand appliqué.

1. Sew B rectangles to opposite sides of the A square. Sew C rectangles to the top and bottom of the unit to make the background block.

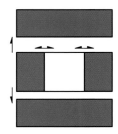

Make 1.

2. For the pieced circles, sew a D square to an E square. Sew a matching F rectangle to the top of the unit. Make four; each unit will be a different color. The units should measure 3½" square.

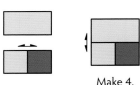

Make 4.

3. Trace four circles onto freezer paper. Cut out each circle. Fold each circle into quarters to establish centering lines.

4. Press a freezer-paper circle on the wrong side of each circle unit, aligning the fold lines with the seams. Using the freezer-paper circle as a guide, cut out each fabric circle, adding ¼" seam allowance. Press the seam allowance under using the edge of the freezer-paper circle as a guide, making sure the edges are smooth.

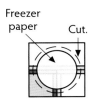

Make 4.

5. Remove the freezer paper. Position the circles on the background block, aligning the seam lines. Appliqué each circle in place.

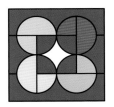

ALTERNATE COLORWAY

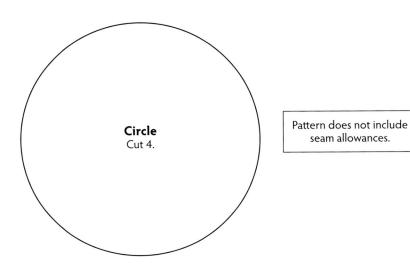

Circle
Cut 4.

Pattern does not include seam allowances.

Rose and Dot

• LORI KENNEDY •

The Rose and Dot block is named after the two lovely ladies who inspired me to sew, my grandmother, Rose, and my mother, Dorothy. They taught me to appreciate the small joys in life, like quilting and gardening. I hope to continue their tradition by sharing this simple flower with future generations of quilters. ~Lori

What You'll Need

A: 1 light blue floral rectangle, 3½" × 6½", for background

B: 1 medium blue stripe rectangle, 3½" × 6½", for background

1 green print square, 5" × 5", for stem and leaves

1 red print square, 4" × 4", for flower

1 yellow print square, 2" × 2", for flower center

1 square of lightweight batting, 3" × 3" (optional)

Template plastic or freezer paper

Appliqué glue

Assembly and Appliqué

Press all seam allowances in the direction indicated by the arrows. The appliqué patterns are on pattern sheet 1. The instructions are written for hand appliqué. The patterns are symmetrical and do not need to be reversed if you prefer to use fusible appliqué.

1. Join the A and B rectangles, right sides together, to make a 6½" square background unit.

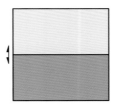

Make 1.

2. Cut a 1" × 3½" strip from the green. Press the strip in half lengthwise with wrong sides together. Open the strip and press each long side toward the center crease to make a ½"-wide stem.

3. Using the patterns, trace one of each shape onto template plastic or freezer paper. Cut out the shapes directly on the line. Use the templates to then cut one flower from the red, one flower center from the yellow, and two leaves from the green, adding a ¼" seam allowance all around.

4. Optional: Cut out flower from batting, cutting directly on the line. On the wrong side of the flower circle, baste or glue the circle of batting in the center of the circle.

5. Position the stem, leaves, flower, and flower center on the background unit, referring to the placement guide and photo. Pin, baste, or glue the pieces to the background and appliqué in place.

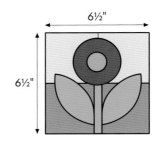

Appliqué placement guide

Free as a Bird

• IRENE BLANCK •

I enjoy sewing with friends, traveling around the world teaching, and meeting new quilters. I named my block Free as a Bird because my quilting career has set me free—traveling to places that I never thought I'd visit. I only started traveling in the last five years, and I've met many wonderful quilters and made many great new friends. ~Irene

What You'll Need

1 cream plaid square, 7" × 7", for background

1 brown print rectangle, 3½" × 4½", for bird body

1 green check rectangle, 2" × 3½", for large wing

1 blue floral square, 4" × 4", for small wing, small tail feather, and small circle

1 red stripe rectangle, 3" × 4", for large tail feather and large circle

1 tan dot rectangle, 2" × 2½", for leaves

1 navy stripe bias strip, 1" × 8", for stem

Template plastic or freezer paper

Brown pearl cotton, size 8, for embroidery

Appliqué

The appliqué patterns are on pattern sheet 1. The instructions are written for needle-turn appliqué (page 135). Reverse the patterns for fusible appliqué.

1. To make the stem, press the navy strip in half lengthwise with wrong sides together. Open the strip and press each long side toward the center crease. Refold along the center crease to make a ¼"-wide stem.

2. Using the patterns, trace one of each shape onto template plastic or freezer paper. Cut out the shapes directly on the line. Use the templates to then cut one of each shape from the chosen fabrics, adding a ¼" seam allowance all around.

3. Referring to the placement guide and photo, position the shapes on the background square in the following order: stem, leaves, tail feathers, bird body, wings, and circles. Pin, baste, or glue the pieces to the background and appliqué in place.

4. Embroider the legs using the pearl cotton and a backstitch. See "Embroidery Stitches" on page 138 for stitching details.

5. Press the block on the wrong side and trim it to 6½" square, keeping the design centered.

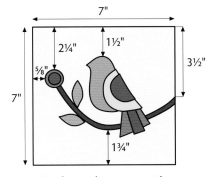

Appliqué placement guide

Snail and Pail

• WENDY SHEPPARD •

This block design was inspired by one of my daughter's treasured childhood playthings—a German watering can in the brightest primary colors. She was fascinated by every garden critter and wildflower (weed!) out there, thus the little snail and little bit of embroidered bloom. ~Wendy

What You'll Need

1 white solid square, 7" × 7", for background

1 blue floral rectangle, 4" × 5", for watering can

1 blue stripe rectangle, 4" × 5", for handle and spout

Scraps of red and yellow prints for snail

Lightweight fusible web, 8" × 8"

Embroidery floss

Appliqué

The appliqué patterns are on pattern sheet 1. The instructions are written for fusible appliqué. If you prefer hand appliqué, reverse the patterns and add a seam allowance.

1. Trace the patterns onto the fusible web, leaving ½" between the shapes. Cut out the shapes, leaving about ¼" outside the drawn lines.

2. Fuse the shapes to the wrong side of the chosen fabrics, following the manufacturer's instructions. Cut out the shapes on the drawn lines and peel away the paper backing.

3. Referring to the appliqué placement guide, position the watering can on the background square. Tuck the ends of the handle under the left side of the can. Position the spout on the opposite side of the can and the snail on the spout. Fuse in place.

4. Stitch around the shapes with a machine blanket stitch to secure the edges of the appliqués.

5. Use two strands of embroidery floss and a backstitch, running stitch, and French knots to embroider the wildflowers and antennae as shown in the photo. See "Embroidery Stitches" on page 138 for stitching details.

6. Press the block on the wrong side and trim it to 6½" square, keeping the design centered.

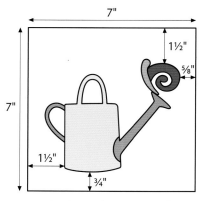

Appliqué placement guide

Quilting Music

· JANE DAVIDSON ·

When I sew, I love to play music. I have a playlist on my computer called "quilting music," a selection of every genre of music that inspires me while sewing: everything from Christmas carols to classical music with a large selection of contemporary rock in the middle. ~Jane

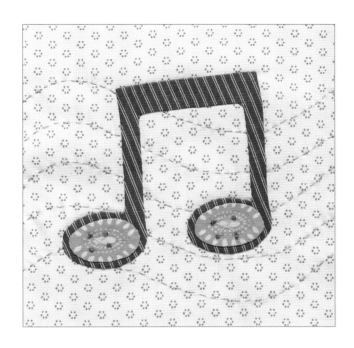

What You'll Need

1 cream print square, 7" × 7", for background

1 red stripe square, 6" × 6", for music note

1 green print square, 4" × 4", for music-note centers

Template plastic or freezer paper

Embroidery floss (blue and yellow)

Appliqué glue

Removable marker

Appliqué

The appliqué patterns are on pattern sheet 1. The instructions are written for hand appliqué. Reverse the patterns for fusible appliqué.

1. Use a removable marker to trace the five-line staff onto the background square.

2. Trace the music note and music-note center patterns onto template plastic or freezer paper. Cut out the shapes directly on the line. Use the templates to then cut one music note from the red and two music-note centers from the green, adding a ¼" seam allowance all around.

3. Position the music note and music-note centers on the background square, referring to the appliqué placement guide and photo. Pin, baste, or glue the pieces to the background and appliqué in place.

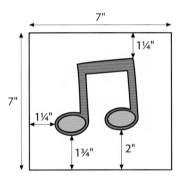

Appliqué placement guide

4. Use two strands of blue floss to embroider a running stitch over the marked five-line staff. See "Embroidery Stitches" on page 138 for stitching details.

5. Using two strands of floss, make four blue French knots and a a yellow cross-stitch in each music-note center.

6. Press the block on the wrong side and trim it to 6½" square, keeping the design centered.

Appliqué and Embroidery Blocks   **61**

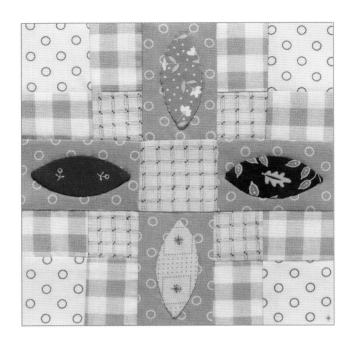

Changing Seasons

• JANE DAVIDSON •

Quilting through the four seasons has always been magical: Snuggling under a warm quilt while sewing a binding in winter or perspiring as you guide the pieces under your sewing machine in the hot, humid summer. Watching the leaves fall as you make your favorite autumn patterns and finding inspiration from the blossoming spring flowers. ~Jane

What You'll Need

A: 4 ivory print squares, 1¾" × 1¾"

B: 8 tan check rectangles, 1½" × 1¾"

1 cream plaid rectangle, 4" × 6"; cut into:

    C: 4 squares, 1½" × 1½"

    D: 1 square, 2" × 2"

E: 4 blue print rectangles, 2" × 2¾"

4 rectangles, 2" × 2½", of assorted prints for leaves

Template plastic or freezer paper

Assembly and Appliqué

Press all seam allowances in the direction indicated by the arrows. The appliqué pattern is on pattern sheet 4. The instructions are written for hand appliqué. The pattern is symmetrical and does not need to be reversed if you prefer to use fusible appliqué.

1. Arrange and sew together one A square, two B rectangles, and one C square to make a four-patch unit as shown. Press. The unit should measure 2¾" square. Make four.

Make 4.

2. Arrange the four-patch units, four E rectangles, and the D square in three rows as shown. Sew the units into rows and press. Join the rows and press to make a 6½" background.

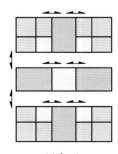

Make 1.

3. Trace the leaf pattern onto template plastic or freezer paper. Cut out the shape directly on the line. Use the template to then cut one leaf each from the four assorted print rectangles, adding a ¼" seam allowance all around.

4. Position the leaves on the block, referring to the appliqué placement guide and photo. Pin, baste, or glue the pieces to the background and appliqué in place.

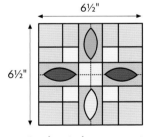

6½"

6½"

Appliqué placement guide

Road Trip

• TERRY ATKINSON •

Follow the open road! In life and in quilting, I never know what's around each bend. When I let the fabric speak to me and I follow the design wherever it leads, I always end up in a happy place. ~Terry

What You'll Need

1 green check square, 7" × 7", for background

1 red stripe rectangle, 4" × 6", for lower camper, hubcap, and wing

1 cream print rectangle, 4" × 6", for upper camper

1 navy print square, 4" × 4", for door and window

1 navy solid square, 2" × 2", for tire

⅛ yard of 17"-wide lightweight fusible web

Appliqué

The appliqué patterns are on pattern sheet 1. The instructions are written for fusible appliqué. If you prefer hand appliqué, reverse the patterns and add a seam allowance.

1. Trace the patterns onto the fusible web, leaving ½" between the shapes. Cut out the shapes, leaving about ¼" outside the drawn lines.

2. Fuse the shapes to the wrong side of the chosen fabrics, following the manufacturer's instructions. Cut out the shapes on the drawn lines and peel away the paper backing.

3. Position the appliqués on the background, referring to the appliqué placement guide and the photo. Fuse in place.

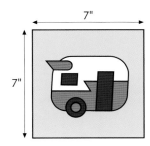

Appliqué placement guide

4. Stitch around the shapes with a machine blanket stitch or zigzag stitch to secure the edges of the appliqués. Press the block on the wrong side and trim it to 6½" square, keeping the design centered.

Hello Sunshine!

• PAT SLOAN •

You'll notice how many of us are inspired by nature. It's amazing to me how much sunshine improves my life. When the sun comes out I feel more alive, more creative, more ready to face wonderful new things. When possible I take long walks. Seeing a blue sky and sunshine fills my soul back up so I'm ready to create again. ~Pat

What You'll Need

1 light blue print square, 7" × 7" for background

1 yellow print square, 6" × 6", for sun rays

7 rectangles, 2" × 5", of assorted yellow prints for sun

Black embroidery floss

Fusible web, 6" × 12"

Paper for foundation piecing

Water-soluble pen

Assembly and Appliqué

The appliqué patterns are on pattern sheet 1. The instructions are written for fusible appliqué. If you prefer hand appliqué, reverse the patterns and add a seam allowance.

1. Trace the sunshine center pattern onto a 5" square of foundation paper.

2. Referring to "Foundation Piecing" on page 136, sew the yellow rectangles to the foundation paper, starting on the lower edge of the sun center. Press and remove the paper.

3. Trace the sun rays pattern and the outer circle of the sun center pattern onto the fusible web, leaving ½" between the shapes. Cut out the shapes, leaving about ¼" outside the drawn lines. Cut out the interior of the shapes, leaving ¼" of fusible web on the inside of the drawn line.

4. Fuse the sun rays to the wrong side of the yellow floral, following the manufacturer's instructions. Fuse the sun center to the wrong side of the pieced unit. Cut out the shapes on the drawn lines.

5. Use a window or light box and a removable marker to draw the smile and eyes on the center. Peel the paper backing from both shapes.

6. Position the rays on the blue square. Place the center on top of the rays. Fuse in place.

7. Stitch around the shapes with a machine blanket stitch to secure.

8. Embroider the smile using two strands of embroidery floss and a stem stitch (page 138). Stitch a French knot for each eye.

9. Press the block on the wrong side and trim it to 6½" square.

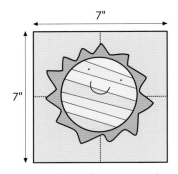

Appliqué placement guide

Nourish

• DEBBIE GRIFKA •

Six days a week, a stack of bowls waits for me to choose one and fill it with my morning oatmeal. Using bold, graphic shapes when I sew reminds me of the simple joys in life—like rich colors and oatmeal for breakfast. ~Debbie

What You'll Need

1 cream print square, 7" × 7", for background

1 red print piece, 2½" × 5", for bowl

1 green print piece, 2½" × 5", for bowl

1 navy print piece, 3" × 5", for bowl

Lightweight fusible web, 5" × 8"

Lightweight stabilizer, 6" × 6" (optional)

Appliqué

The appliqué patterns are on pattern sheet 1. The instructions are written for fusible appliqué. If you prefer hand appliqué, reverse the patterns and add a seam allowance.

1. Trace the patterns onto the fusible web, leaving ½" between the shapes. Cut out the shapes, leaving ¼" outside the drawn lines.

2. Fuse the shapes to the wrong side of the chosen fabrics,

following the manufacturer's instructions. Cut out the shapes on the drawn lines and peel away the paper backing.

3. Starting with the top bowl, position the bowls on the background square, referring to the appliqué placement guide and the photo. Fuse in place.

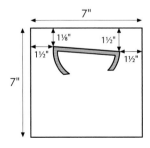

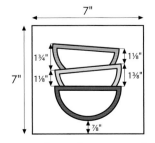

Appliqué placement guide

4. Pin the stabilizer to the back of the square (optional). Using matching threads and a machine satin stitch, sew around the outer and inner edges of each bowl.

5. Press the block on the wrong side and trim it to 6½" square, keeping the design centered.

Potted Paisleys

• AMY K. JOHNSON •

I enjoy quilting my quilts. Swirling and swooshing around on my projects lets the worries of the day evaporate. One of my favorite quilting designs is the paisley, so I decided to re-create some in appliqué and stitch a pot of paisleys! ~Amy

What You'll Need

1 cream print square, 7" × 7", for background

1 navy stripe piece, 5" × 6", for paisleys

1 blue floral piece, 3" × 5", for paisley centers and bud

1 red print piece, 3" × 4" for flower pot

1 green print piece, 2" × 4", for leaves

Lightweight fusible web, 9" × 10"

Green embroidery floss or 28-weight thread

Appliqué

The appliqué patterns are on pattern sheet 1. The instructions are written for fusible appliqué. If you prefer hand appliqué, reverse the patterns and add a seam allowance.

1. Trace the patterns onto the fusible web, leaving ½" between the shapes. Cut out the shapes, leaving about ¼" outside the drawn lines.

2. Fuse the shapes to the wrong side of the chosen fabrics, following the manufacturer's instructions. Cut out the shapes on the drawn lines and peel away the paper backing.

3. Referring to the appliqué placement guide and the photo, position the pieces on the background square. Fuse the appliqués in place.

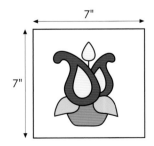

Appliqué placement guide

4. Embroider the stem using two strands of embroidery floss or 28-weight thread and a backstitch. See "Embroidery Stitches" on page 138 for stitching details.

5. Stitch around the shapes with a machine blanket stitch to secure the edges of the appliqués. Press the block on the wrong side and trim it to 6½" square, keeping the design centered.

SWITCH THE STITCHES

If your machine doesn't have a built-in blanket stitch, you can use a narrow zigzag stitch—or blanket stitch the edges by hand.

Trip to the Quilt Shop

• LAURA KAY HOUSER •

One of my favorite patterns is the classic Trip around the World. When Pat asked me to participate in this project, I immediately thought of my travels. Not only the traveling I do for work and fun, but about all the quilters that come to visit my shop from near and far. ~Laura Kay

What You'll Need

A: 1 cream print square, 1½" × 1½"

B: 4 red print squares, 1½" × 1½"

C: 8 navy print squares, 1½" × 1½"

D: 8 blue print squares, 1½" × 1½"

E: 4 green print squares, 1½" × 1½"

1 yellow print piece, 5" × 8";

   cut into:

   F: 2 strips, 1½" × 5½"

   G: 2 strips, 1½" × 7"

Variegated red embroidery floss

Assembly and Embroidery

Press all seam allowances in the direction indicated by the arrows. For embroidery techniques and stitch detail, refer to "Embroidery Basics" on page 138.

1. Arrange the A–E squares in five rows as shown. Sew the squares together into rows and press. Join the rows and press. The block center should measure 5½" square.

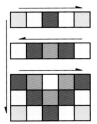

2. Sew the F strips to the top and bottom of the block center and press. Sew the G strips to the sides of the block. Press.

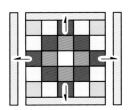

3. Trace the embroidery pattern on pattern sheet 1 onto the border and center square as shown in the photo. Make sure the embroidery is near the inner edge of the border, as you will be trimming the outer edge after embroidery is complete.

4. Embroider the design using two strands of embroidery floss and a backstitch. Press the block, and then trim it to 6½" square, keeping the design centered.

Blue Ribbon

• MELISSA MORTENSON •

I moved to Kentucky in my early twenties and immediately fell in love with the hoopla surrounding the Kentucky Derby. I cherished not only the event itself but all of the traditions as well. Ribbons are not awarded at the Derby but are frequently associated with horse competitions. To me a Dresden block always looked a bit like a prize ribbon. ~Melissa

What You'll Need

A: 1 cream print square, 7" × 7", for background

B: 1 navy print square, 5" × 5", for Dresden blades

C: 1 blue print square, 5" × 5", for Dresden blades

D: 1 green print square, 5" × 5", for Dresden blades

E: 2 tan check squares, 5" × 5", for center circle

F: 1 navy-and-blue rectangle, 5" × 6", for ribbon

Template plastic

Appliqué glue

Navy embroidery floss

Dresden Plate Preparation

Press all seam allowances in the direction indicated by the arrows.

1. Make a template for the Dresden blade using the pattern on page 69 and template plastic. Trace the template seven times on each of the B and C squares and six times on the D square. Cut out along the marked lines.

2. Fold a blade in half lengthwise, right sides together. Finger-press to crease and sew a scant ¼" seam across the top. Carefully clip the top corner, leaving a few thread widths beyond the stitched line.

Trim.
Fold.

3. Finger-press the seam open. Turn to the right side and gently push out the point. Align the seam with the center crease and press flat. Make 20 Dresden blades.

Make 20.

4. Begin sewing at the inner (flat) edge of the blade. Sew the blades together in sets of five. Join two sets together to make a half circle; sew the halves together. Press.

Ribbon and Circle Preparation

1. Make a template for the ribbon using the pattern on page 69 and template plastic. Trace the template two times on the wrong side of the F rectangle. Cut out along the marked lines.

2. Fold a ribbon in half, right sides together. Stitch down the side and across the bottom of the ribbon, starting and stopping with a backstitch. Leave the top edge open. Turn to the right side and gently push out the point.

Fold.

Make 2.

3. Make a template for the center circle using the pattern below and template plastic. Trace the circle onto the wrong side of one E square. Place the E squares right sides together with the marked circle on top. Sew on the marked line. Cut out the circles, adding ¼" outside the stitching. Clip the seam allowance, making sure to not clip the stitched line.

4. Cut a slit in the back of one circle. Turn the circles right side out through the slit. Smooth out the edges and press.

Assembly and Appliqué

Refer to the photo for placement guidance as needed.

1. Fold the A square in half in both directions and finger-press. Place a ribbon on the A square with the angled edge about ⅝" from the bottom edge of the square and the raw edges touching the center crease. Repeat, placing the other ribbon on the opposite side of the center crease. Glue the ribbons in place.

2. Glue the Dresden plate on the A square, aligning the points of the blades with the creases. Stitch around the shapes using a machine blanket stitch.

3. Glue the circle in the center of the Dresden plate. Use three strands of embroidery floss and a running stitch to secure the circle just inside the edge. See "Embroidery Stitches" on page 138 for stitching details.

4. Press the block on the wrong side and trim it to 6½" square, keeping the design centered.

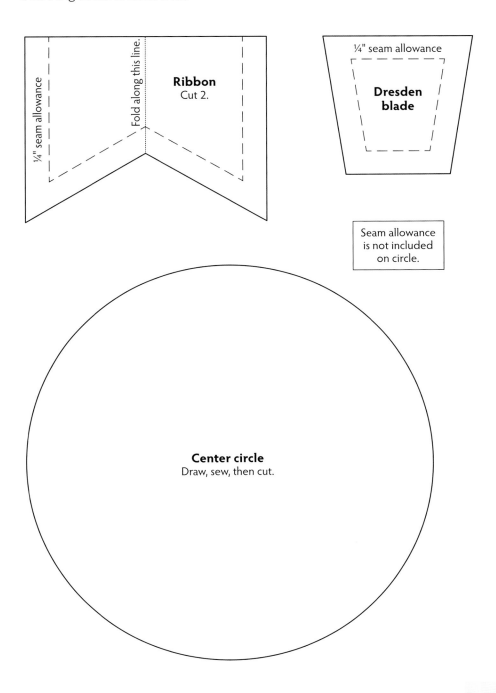

¼" seam allowance

Fold along this line.

Ribbon
Cut 2.

¼" seam allowance

Dresden blade

Seam allowance is not included on circle.

Center circle
Draw, sew, then cut.

Stitch 'N' Paws

• RICHY LAINSON, JR. •

I spent hundreds of hours stitching with my dachshund, Miss V, who passed away last May. She filled me with joy and love. She loved to curl up with me while I appliquéd and I deeply miss that. This block represents my quilting life with V, for nothing was as splendid as stitching with her by my side. ~Richy

What You'll Need

1 cream solid square, 10" × 10", cut into:

    A: 1 square, 5" × 5"

    B: 2 strips, 1" × 5½"

    C: 2 strips, 1" × 6½"

1 blue print piece, 4" × 6"; cut into:

    D: 2 strips, ¾" × 5"

    E: 2 strips, ¾" × 5½"

1 red print square, 6" × 6", for paws

1 green print square, 6" × 6", for leaves

Lightweight fusible interfacing, 6½" × 6½"

Template plastic or freezer paper

Embroidery floss: red, blue, navy, dark green, light green

Basic embroidery supplies (page 138)

Assembly and Appliqué

The appliqué and embroidery patterns are on page 71. The instructions are written for needle-turn appliqué. Reverse the patterns for fusible appliqué. Press all seam allowances in the direction indicated by the arrows. Refer to "Embroidery Basics" on page 138 as needed.

1. Sew the D strips to the top and bottom of the A square. Sew the E strips to opposite sides. Press. Sew the B strips to the top and bottom of the unit. Sew the C strips to opposite sides. Press. The block should measure 6½" square.

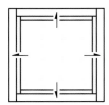

2. Trace the embroidery pattern onto the block; use a small dot to mark the French knots and lazy daisies.

3. Trace the leaves and paw prints onto the template plastic or freezer paper and cut out. Use the templates to prepare the paw and leaf appliqués.

4. Using the photo as a guide, position the appliqué shapes on the block. Pin or baste in place. Stitch the appliqué shapes by hand using an appliqué stitch.

5. Fuse the interfacing to the wrong side of the block. Embroider the design using two strands of embroidery floss. Refer to the block photo for colors and the embroidery key on page 71 for stitches to use.

6. Press the block gently on the wrong side after the embroidery is complete.

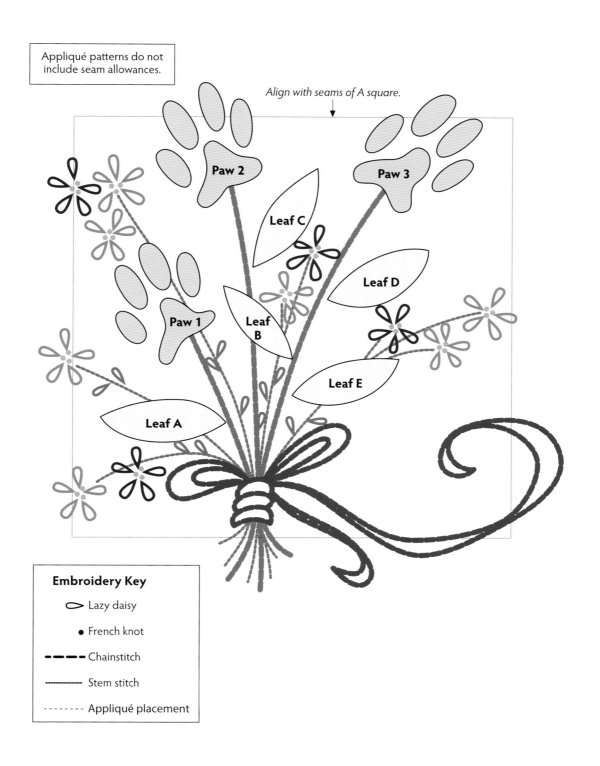

Appliqué patterns do not include seam allowances.

Align with seams of A square.

Paw 2

Paw 3

Leaf C

Leaf D

Paw 1

Leaf B

Leaf E

Leaf A

Embroidery Key

⬭ Lazy daisy

● French knot

▬ ▬ ▬ Chainstitch

———— Stem stitch

- - - - - - Appliqué placement

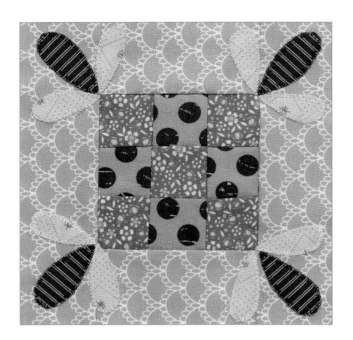

For Madge

• PAT SLOAN •

My mother-in-law, Madge, is a beautiful seamstress. She taught me a lot about sewing clothing and has been a great encourager. I challenged her to learn to quilt, which created a wonderful new bond for us as we learned together and continue to share a love of quilts. Madge's first sampler contained a Honeybee block, which I've always loved. ~Pat

What You'll Need

A: 5 red print squares, 1½" × 1½"

B: 4 tan dot squares, 1½" × 1½"

1 tan print piece, 5" × 8"; cut into:
    C: 2 strips, 2" × 3½"
    D: 2 strips, 2" × 6½"

E: 1 navy stripe rectangle, 3" × 5", for bee bodies

F: 1 yellow print square, 5" × 5", for bee wings

Lightweight fusible web, 5" × 8"

Assembly and Appliqué

Press all seam allowances in the direction indicated by the arrows. The appliqué patterns are on pattern sheet 2. The instructions are written for fusible appliqué. If you prefer hand appliqué, add a seam allowance as you cut the appliqués.

1. Arrange the A and B squares in three rows. Sew the squares together into rows and press. Join the rows and press. The nine-patch unit should measure 3½" square.

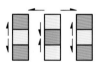

2. Sew the C strips to the top and bottom of the unit and press. Sew the D strips to the sides of the block. Press to make a 6½" block.

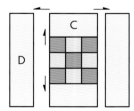

3. Trace four bee bodies onto the fusible web, leaving ½" between the shapes. Trace eight bee wings onto the fusible web, leaving ½" between the shapes. Cut out the shapes, leaving about ¼" outside the drawn lines.

4. Fuse the bee bodies to the wrong side of the navy stripe, following the manufacturer's instructions. Fuse the bee wings to the wrong side of the yellow print. Cut out the shapes on the drawn lines and peel away the paper backing.

5. Position a bee body and two wings in each corner, referring to the appliqué placement guide and photo. Fuse in place. Stitch around each shape using a machine blanket stitch to secure the edges. Press from the wrong side.

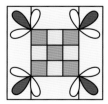

Appliqué placement guide

Clamshells

• HELEN STUBBINGS •

When I'm stitching, I turn off my mind and exist in my own little world. No distractions, no worries, no pressures, just me and my needle. Bonuses may include stitching friends, cocktails by the pool, or a glorious garden on a sunny spring day with everything I need right by my side. Oh, and did I mention chocolate? Of course chocolate always helps! ~Helen

What You'll Need

1 square, 7" × 7", of cream print for background

1 square, 3" × 3", of 10 assorted prints for clamshells

1 square, 7" × 7", of lightweight fusible stabilizer

Embroidery floss (pink, blue, and green)

Template plastic, cardstock, fabric glue stick, and appliqué glue

Basic embroidery supplies (page 138)

Embroidery and Assembly

For embroidery techniques and stitch detail, refer to "Embroidery Basics" on page 138.

1. Using a light box or window, trace the pattern on pattern sheet 2 onto the background fabric. Fuse the stabilizer on the wrong side of the block.

2. Embroider the design using two strands of floss. Use a stem stitch for stems and flower centers, a backstitch for petals, and a lazy daisy for leaves.

3. Make a plastic template using the clamshell pattern on pattern sheet 2. Trace 10 clamshells onto cardstock and cut out.

4. Trace a clamshell on the wrong side of each 3" square. Cut out, adding a generous ¼" seam allowance all around.

5. Center a cardstock template on the wrong side of a fabric clamshell. Using the fabric glue stick, apply glue along the top curved edge of the template. Finger-press the seam allowance onto the glue, using small pinches to make a smooth curve. Repeat to glue baste all of the clamshells.

6. Lay out the clamshells in three rows. Hand stitch the clamshells where the edges meet. Make two rows with three clamshells and one row with four clamshells.

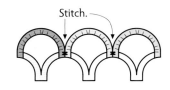

Make 2.

Make 1.

7. Position the clamshell rows on the background. Dot appliqué glue on the seam allowance to hold the rows together. Appliqué along the top of each row, starting with the top row. Remove the cardstock before stitching the next row.

8. Press the block on the wrong side and trim it to 6½" square.

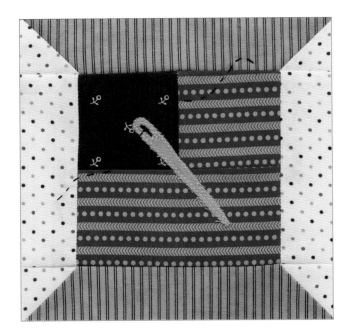

American Spool

• TAMMY VONDERSCHMITT •

I graduated high school in 1976, and my school's colors were red, white, and blue. I've always been partial to the flag symbol and what it means. And I started sewing when I was a small child so I've always had needle and thread in my possession. Today I still decorate my home with Americana—and I still love my needle and thread. ~Tammy

What You'll Need

1 cream print piece, 4" × 7";
  cut into:
  A: 4 squares, 1½" × 1½"
  B: 2 rectangles, 1½" × 4½"
C: 2 blue stripe rectangles,
  1½" × 6½"
D: 1 navy print square, 2½" × 2½"
1 red stripe piece, 3" × 8"; cut into:
  E: 1 square, 2½" × 2½"
  F: 1 rectangle, 2½" × 4½"
1 gold solid square, 3" × 3",
  for needle
Lightweight fusible web, 3" × 3"
Navy pearl cotton or 12-weight
  cotton thread

Assembly and Appliqué

Press all seam allowances in the direction indicated by the arrows. The appliqué pattern is on page 75. The instructions are written for fusible appliqué. If you prefer hand appliqué, and add a seam allowance when you cut the appliqué.

1. Draw a diagonal line from corner to corner on the wrong side of the A squares.

2. Referring to "Stitch and Flip" on page 137, sew two marked A squares to each C rectangle to make two units.

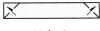

Make 2.

3. Sew together the D square, E square, and F rectangle to make the block center. The unit should measure 4½" square.

4. Orient the block center with the D square in the upper-left corner. Sew the B rectangles to the sides of the block center and press. Sew the units from step 2 to the top and bottom and press to make a 6½" block.

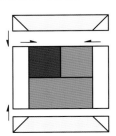

5. Trace the needle pattern onto the fusible web. Cut out the shape, leaving about ¼" outside the drawn line. Fuse the shape to the wrong side of the gold square, following the manufacturer's instructions. Cut out the shape on the drawn line and peel away the paper backing.

6. Place the needle on the block, referring to the photo for placement. Stitch around the shape using a machine blanket stitch to secure the edges. Press the block on the wrong side.

7. Use pearl cotton or 12-weight thread and a running stitch to embroider the line of thread.

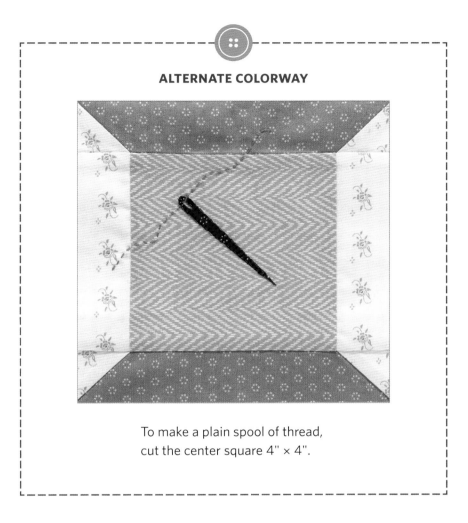

ALTERNATE COLORWAY

To make a plain spool of thread, cut the center square 4" × 4".

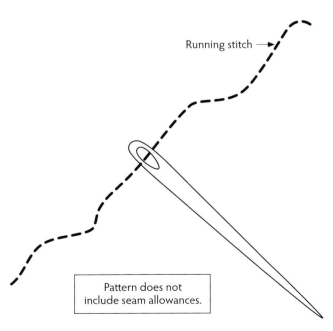

Running stitch →

Pattern does not include seam allowances.

Quilt Love

• PAT SLOAN •

I wear my heart on my sleeve. I also use lots of hearts in the things I make and the notes I write, and I'm fond of saying that I LOVE this or that. Because I do, I really do, love many things! When I made my first quilt, I fell in love with fabric all over again. I could create images and feelings using the fabric as my paint. Quilting has stolen my heart again and again, and every time I stitch, my heart soars! ~Pat

What You'll Need

1 blue print square, 7" × 7", for background

1 red floral rectangle, 4" × 6", for heart

1 red print rectangle, 4" × 6", for heart

1 white print rectangle, 4" × 6", for letters

Lightweight fusible web, 6" × 12"

Appliqué

The appliqué patterns are on pattern sheet 3. The instructions are written for fusible appliqué. If you prefer hand appliqué, reverse the patterns and add a seam allowance.

1. Trace the patterns onto the fusible web, leaving ½" between the shapes. Cut out the shapes, leaving about ¼" outside the drawn lines. For the heart shapes only, cut out the interior of the heart, leaving ¼" of fusible web on the inside of the line.

2. Fuse the shapes to the wrong side of the chosen fabrics, following the manufacturer's instructions. Cut out the shapes on the drawn lines and peel away the paper backing.

3. Position the heart shapes in the center of the background square, slightly overlapping them in the center. Position the letters on top of the heart. Fuse in place.

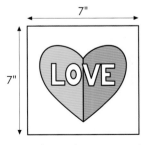

Appliqué placement guide

SHADOWING TIP

If you can see the red fabric through the white appliquéd letters, that's shadowing. To avoid shadowing, make a second tracing of the letters, fuse them to white solid or muslin, and cut them out. Fuse the white or muslin letters to the background fabric first, then layer the final fabric letters on top and fuse them. Finally, stitch through both layers at the same time.

4. Stitch around the shapes with a machine blanket stitch to secure the edges of the appliqués. Press the block on the wrong side and trim it to 6½" square, keeping the design centered.

Sunbonnet Me to You

· JANE DAVIDSON ·

For me, making and giving away quilts has always been the most rewarding part of being a quilter. Quilting is a craft of love, given from the heart to provide warmth and comfort and to create memories. ~Jane

What You'll Need

1 light print square, 7" × 7", for background

Scraps of assorted prints for sleeves, hands, dress, legs, boots, hat, hatband, quilt, and heart

Template plastic or freezer paper

Embroidery floss (navy and light blue)

Appliqué glue

Water-soluble pen

Appliqué

The appliqué patterns are on pattern sheet 1. The instructions are written for hand appliqué. Reverse the patterns for fusible appliqué.

1. Make templates from plastic or freezer paper using the patterns.

2. Prepare the appliqué pieces by tracing around the templates on the right side of the chosen fabrics. Cut out, adding a scant ¼" seam allowance all around.

3. Position the shapes on the background square in the following order: back leg and boot, front leg and boot, back sleeve and hand, dress, front sleeve, quilt, front hand, hat, hatband, and heart. Stitch the appliqué shapes by hand using an appliqué stitch.

4. Embroider the ground using a backstitch and two strands of embroidery floss; refer to "Embroidery Stitches" on page 138 for stitching instructions.

5. Trace the word *Gift* onto the heart. Use a backstitch and two strands of embroidery floss to embroider the word. Add French knots to the beginning and end of each letter.

6. Press the block on the wrong side and trim it to 6½" square, keeping the design centered.

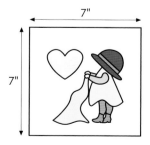

Appliqué placement guide

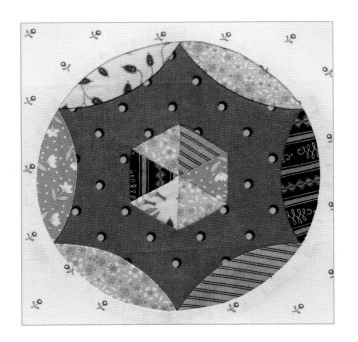

Full Circle

• MISSIE CARPENTER •

I love stitching challenging projects that become less challenging as I work on them. The shapes in this block used to be challenging for me. But as I've sewn these shapes, my starch basting for English paper piecing and appliqué techniques have improved my hand piecing. The stress is gone, and it's relaxing to know I'm stitching my best quilts. ~Missie

What You'll Need

A: 1 square, 7" × 7", of cream print for background

B: 1 square, 7" × 7", of red print for star

C: 1 rectangle, 4" × 6", of yellow print for petals and triangles

D: 4 squares, 4" × 4", of different prints for petals and triangles

Freezer paper, spray starch, appliqué glue, and small paintbrush

Template Preparation

1. Using the pattern on pattern sheet 2, carefully trace six triangles and six petals onto freezer paper. Cut a second piece of freezer paper the same size as the traced piece. Press the waxy side of the traced freezer paper to the *dull side* of the second piece of freezer paper. *Do not* press waxy side to waxy side. Cut out the paper triangles and petals.

2. Carefully trace the star shape onto freezer paper. Press the waxy side of the traced freezer paper to the *dull side* of a second piece of freezer paper. Cut out the star shape and the hexagon from the center.

3. Cut two 7" square pieces of freezer paper. Trace the background circle in the center of one piece. Press the waxy side of the traced freezer paper to the *dull side* of the second square of freezer paper. Cut out the center circle and set it aside for another project or discard.

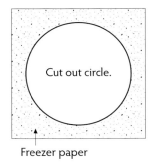

Cut out circle.

Freezer paper

Triangle and Petal Preparation

1. Press the waxy side of two paper triangles and two paper petals to the wrong side of the C rectangle. Press the waxy side of one triangle and one petal to the wrong side of each D square. Cut around each shape, adding a ¼" seam allowance.

2. Spray some starch into the lid of the spray can and use a small paintbrush to apply it to the seam allowance on two sides of each triangle. Fold the edges of the fabric over the edges of the freezer-paper template. Using a medium-hot iron, press the seam allowance over the freezer-paper template on two sides of each triangle. Or use a needle and thread to baste the fabric to the paper as described in "English Paper Piecing" on page 136.

3. Apply starch and press the seam allowance over the freezer-paper template along one curved edge only on each petal. *Do not press the seam allowance over the paper along the second curved edge.*

Assembly and Appliqué

1. Referring to "English Paper Piecing" on page 136, whipstitch the triangles together along the folded edges to make two sets of three. Sew the two halves together to make the block center. The raw edges of each triangle will be at the outer edge of the hexagon you're forming.

2. Fold the paper star shape in half in both directions and press. Fold the B square in half in both directions and finger-press. Use the creases to center the paper star shape, waxy side down, on the right side of the B square and press.

3. Apply small dots of glue to the folded seam allowance of each petal. Position the petals on the B square, using the paper star shape as a guide and placing the folded edge of the petal next to the paper shape. Appliqué the petals in place along the folded edges. Remove the paper star shape from the right side of the B square.

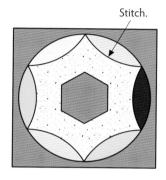

Stitch.

4. Center the paper star shape, waxy side down, on the wrong side of the B square, aligning the outer edges of the freezer-paper template with the stitched line of the petals. Press in place. Cut out the center hexagon shape, adding a ¼" seam allowance. Clip the seam allowance. Apply starch to the seam allowance. Press the seam allowance over the paper template to the back.

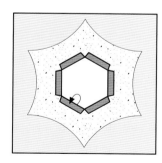

5. Apply small dots of glue to the seam allowance on the pieced hexagon. Place the unit from step 4 on top of the hexagon unit, right side up, and align the points of the hexagon shape with the seams. Appliqué in place.

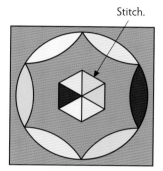

Stitch.

6. Press the paper background square (with cutout circle) to the wrong side of the A square. Mark the center circle and then cut out the circle, adding a ¼" seam allowance inside the marked line. Clip the seam allowance. Apply starch and press the seam allowance over the paper template. Allow the piece to cool and then carefully remove the freezer paper.

7. Glue the background fabric on top of the appliquéd unit, making sure to cover the outer edges of the petals. Appliqué in place. Trim the B square from underneath the A square, leaving a ¼" seam allowance.

8. Press the block on the wrong side and trim it to 6½" square, keeping the design centered.

Fruit Bowl

· JO AVERY ·

I love making quilts that remind me of my garden and reflect my love of nature. It was harvest time at home in Scotland when I was designing this block, and I was busy collecting plums and apples from our orchard. The fall harvest inspired my design for a fruit bowl that uses both piecing and appliqué. ~Jo

What You'll Need

1 cream print square, 6½" × 6½"; cut into:
  A: 1 rectangle, 3¼" × 6½" (set aside remainder for concave shapes)

1 navy print piece, 4" × 8"; cut into:
  B: 1 strip, 1½" × 3" (set aside remainder for 2 convex shapes)

C: 1 blue print strip, 1¼" × 6½"

Scraps of assorted red, green, and yellow prints for circle appliqués

Template plastic

Freezer paper

Appliqué and Assembly

The appliqué patterns are on page 81. The instructions are written for hand appliqué. The patterns are symmetrical and do not need to be reversed if you prefer to use fusible appliqué. Press all seam allowances in the direction indicated by the arrows.

1. Trace three large circles and two small circles onto the dull side of freezer paper. Cut out the circles on the traced lines. Press the large and small circles onto the wrong side of the chosen prints, leaving at least ⅝" between them. Cut out the circles, adding a generous ¼" seam allowance.

2. Sew a gathering stitch (long running stitch; page 138) around the edges of a large circle on the right side of the fabric, about ¼" in from the edge. Don't knot the start or end; instead leave a long thread tail at both ends.

3. Gently pull the thread tails to gather the fabric over the freezer-paper template until it's evenly gathered and taut around the edge of the circle. Smooth out any puckers on the edge. Tie off the threads to hold the gathering firmly in place. Press well. Repeat for the other four circles.

4. Gently remove the freezer paper. Tighten the gathering stitches if required to reshape the circle. Repeat for each circle.

5. Position the large and small circles on the A rectangle, referring to the appliqué placement guide and photo. Appliqué in place. Use a rotary cutter and ruler to trim the bottom of the circles even with the edge of the A rectangle.

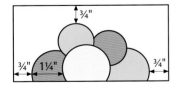

Appliqué placement guide

6. Make plastic templates using the concave and convex patterns below. Trace and cut two convex quarter circles from the remaining navy print. Trace and cut two concave corner pieces from the remaining cream print.

7. Place a concave piece right sides together on a convex piece (the curves will be facing opposite directions). Pin the center point, and then pin the two ends. Ease in the remaining edges and pin. Sew slowly using a ¼" seam allowance and removing the pins as you sew. Press. The unit should measure 3" square. Make two units.

Make 2.

8. Arrange and sew the pieced units and B strip together as shown to make the bottom row.

9. Sew the C strip between the appliquéd rectangle and the bottom row as shown. Press. The block should measure 6½" square.

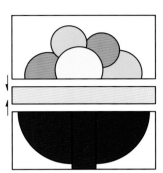

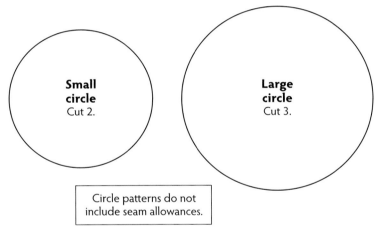

Small circle
Cut 2.

Large circle
Cut 3.

Circle patterns do not include seam allowances.

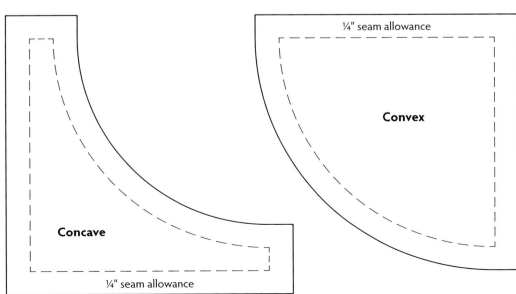

¼" seam allowance

Convex

Concave

¼" seam allowance

Let's Go Sew!

• PAT SLOAN •

One of the very first crafts I taught myself, after creating beaded necklaces, was embroidery. I still have my bright plastic embroidery basket from the '70s, with a fabric drawstring top. Adding embroidery makes a project come alive. It might be a whole block like this one, or just a few added touches like others in this book. The slow rhythm of taking stitches by hand is so calming. ~Pat

What You'll Need

1 square, 7" × 7", of cream print for background

1 square, 7" × 7", of lightweight fusible interfacing

12-weight cotton embroidery thread or embroidery floss: green, red, navy

Basic embroidery supplies (page 138)

Embroidery

For embroidery techniques and stitch detail, refer to "Embroidery Basics" on page 138.

1. Using a light box or window, trace the pattern on pattern sheet 2 onto the background fabric.

2. Embroider the design using one strand of 12-weight thread or two strands of embroidery floss. Use a stem stitch for the solid lines and a French knot for the dots.

3. Press the block on the wrong side and trim it to 6½" square, keeping the design centered.

STABILIZE YOUR STITCHES

Using a lightweight stabilizer on the back of your embroidery keeps it nice and flat. See "Transferring the Design" on page 138 for more information.

Octopus

• ROB APPELL •

The fabric for this project arrived as I was on my way to catch a flight to Hawaii, where I was to teach for a week and be a guest artist at the Tropical Inspirations Quilt Show in Kona. My family had a blast traveling to such a beautiful place. I was in Hawaii for work, but back in the studio I took a second look at these fun prints and saw an octopus, so I started to appliqué. ~Rob

What You'll Need

1 navy print square, 7" × 7", for background

Scraps of assorted prints for octopus, tentacles, eyes, underwater plants, and bubbles

Lightweight fusible web

Appliqué

The appliqué patterns are on pattern sheet 2. The instructions are written for fusible appliqué. If you prefer hand appliqué, reverse the patterns and add a seam allowance.

1. Trace the patterns onto the fusible web, leaving ½" between the shapes. Cut out the shapes, leaving about ¼" outside the drawn lines.

2. Fuse the shapes to the wrong side of the chosen fabrics, following the manufacturer's instructions. Cut out the shapes on the drawn lines and peel away the paper backing.

3. Referring to the appliqué placement guide and the photo, position the pieces on the background square, keeping a ¼" margin around the outer edges. Fuse the appliqués in place.

Appliqué placement guide

4. Using matching thread and a straight stitch, sew around the outer edges of the appliqué shapes.

5. Press the block on the wrong side and trim it to 6½" square, keeping the design centered.

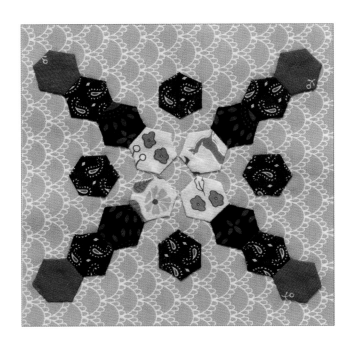

Lots o' Hexies

• YVONNE BUSDEKER •

Hexies were the first thing I learned to stitch when introduced to English paper piecing. I instantly fell in love with the relaxation of hand stitching. The quiet downtime is something I look forward to among my life's chaos. ~Yvonne

What You'll Need

A: 1 tan print square, 7" × 7", for background

B: 1 navy paisley piece, 5" × 6", for hexagons

C: 1 navy print square, 4" × 4", for hexagons

D: 1 light blue print square, 4" × 4", for hexagons

E: 1 red print square, 4" × 4", for hexagons

Template plastic

Cardstock for English-paper-piecing foundations

Fabric glue stick

Assembly

1. Make a plastic template using the pattern on page 85. Trace 20 hexagons onto cardstock and cut out exactly on the drawn lines.

2. Trace eight hexagons on the wrong side of the B piece. Cut out, adding a generous ¼" seam allowance all around. Repeat to cut four hexagons each from the C, D, and E squares.

3. Center a cardstock template on the wrong side of a fabric hexagon. Apply a line of glue on the template near the edge. Finger-press the seam allowance onto the glue line and hold for a moment to secure. Continue in the same way until all the seam allowances are glue basted to the template.

Apply glue.

4. Using a very small whipstitch (page 136), sew one edge of an E hexagon to a B hexagon, taking care to not sew through the paper. Start and finish with a knot. In the same way, add a C hexagon, and then a D hexagon. Make four hexagon units.

Make 4.

5. Press the four hexagon units and remaining four single hexagons and carefully remove the cardstock. If necessary, use a dab of glue to hold tails and seam allowances in place.

6. Fold the A square in half vertically, horizontally, and diagonally to create creases for the hexagon placement. Position the hexagon units on the diagonal lines. Place the remaining hexagons on the vertical and horizontal lines as shown. Secure with glue and appliqué the hexagons to the background.

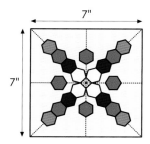

Appliqué placement guide

7. Press the block on the wrong side and trim it to 6½" square, keeping the design centered.

Hexagon
Make 20.

ALTERNATE COLORWAY

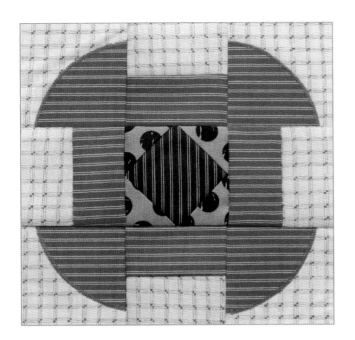

Sewing Circle

• ANDY KNOWLTON •

I have a circle of friends whom I love and admire. We get together when we can, but we're all busy moms, so it can be difficult. Like the divided circle in this block, we're often separated by our other responsibilities, but stay connected by our friendship (and through lots of texting!).
~Andy

What You'll Need

1 red print square, 7" × 7"; cut into:
- **A:** 1 square, 5" × 5"
- **B:** 4 rectangles, 1½" × 2½" (for directional fabrics, cut 2 lengthwise and 2 crosswise)

1 light print square, 7" × 7"; cut into:
- **C:** 1 square, 5" × 5"
- **D:** 4 rectangles, 1½" × 2½"

E: 1 navy square, 2½" × 2½"
F: 4 polka dot squares, 1½" × 1½"
Lightweight fusible web, 5" × 5"

Assembly

Press all seam allowances in the direction indicated by the arrows.

1. Referring to "Stitch and Flip" on page 137, sew the F squares to the E square.

2. Sew each B rectangle to a D rectangle to make four units that measure 2½" square.

Make 4.

3. Trace the circle pattern on pattern sheet 2 onto the fusible web. Cut out the circle, leaving about ¼" outside the drawn lines. Fuse the circle to the wrong side of the A square, following the manufacturer's instructions. Cut out the circle on the marked line. Peel away the paper backing.

4. Fold the A circle and C square in half in both directions and finger-press. Use the creases to center the circle on the C square and fuse it in place. Stitch around the circle using matching thread and a narrow zigzag to secure the edges.

5. Cut the appliquéd square in half in both directions to make four squares that measure 2½" × 2½".

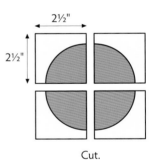

Cut.

6. Arrange and sew the pieced units in rows as shown. Press. Sew the rows together to make a 6½" block. Press.

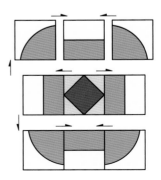

Making Templates

• JANE DAVIDSON •

The first quilt I ever made used a block that had 13 pieces. I remember drawing the block and making all the templates from plastic. I still have the original templates in a box to remind me of my first quilt and how anything worthwhile takes time and effort. ~Jane

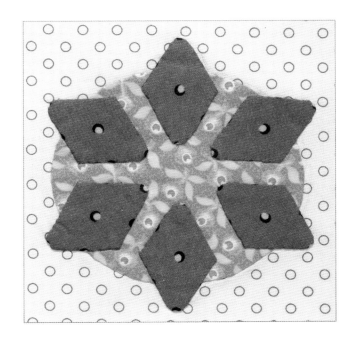

What You'll Need

1 light print square, 7" × 7", for background

1 green print square, 6" × 6", for oval

1 red print rectangle, 6" × 8", for diamonds

Template plastic or freezer paper

Appliqué glue

Water-soluble pen

Appliqué

The appliqué patterns are on pattern sheet 2. The instructions are written for needle-turn appliqué (page 135).

1. Using the water-soluble pen, trace the oval and diamonds onto the background square.

2. Make templates from plastic or freezer paper using the patterns.

3. Prepare the appliqué pieces by tracing around the templates on the right side of the chosen fabrics. Cut out, adding a scant ¼" seam allowance all around.

4. Position the oval on the background square and appliqué in place, turning under the seam allowance on the marked line. Position and appliqué the diamonds in place in the same manner.

5. Press the block on the wrong side and trim it to 6½" square, keeping the design centered.

STITCH SOMETHING NEW!

We all have favorite sewing techniques. Try something new and you may find you love it!

My Happy Place

• PAT SLOAN •

Being a technology focused quilter, I love my modern sewing machine. Sitting down in my studio, with a stack of fabric all cut out and ready to sew, is my happy place. I love all the bells and whistles my modern machine has. I love how efficient I am when I sew with her. And I really love to hear her hum along as I make quilt after quilt after quilt. ~Pat

What You'll Need

1 cream print square, 7" × 7", for background

1 red floral rectangle, 4" × 5", for sewing machine

2½" × 2½" squares of assorted prints:

    1 red and 1 yellow for scissors

    1 white for ruler

    1 yellow check for sewing-machine panel

    4 assorted blues for bulletin board and spool

    1 navy floral for triangle

1 brown print rectangle, 4" × 6", for table and spool ends

1 tan print rectangle, 3" × 6", for bulletin board

1 navy print strip, 2½" × 3½", for sewing-machine panel

Lightweight fusible web, 5" × 12"

12-weight cotton thread or embroidery floss: navy, blue

Appliqué

The appliqué patterns are on pattern sheet 2. The instructions are written for fusible appliqué. If you prefer hand appliqué, reverse the patterns and add a seam allowance.

1. Trace the patterns onto the fusible web, leaving ½" between the shapes. Cut out the shapes, leaving about ¼" outside the drawn lines.

2. Fuse the shapes to the wrong side of the chosen fabrics, following the manufacturer's instructions.

3. Since most of the pieces are small, wait to cut out the shapes on the drawn lines until you're ready to position them on the background square. Peel away the paper backing after cutting out each shape.

4. Fuse the bulletin board, sewing machine, and table on the background square. Fuse the ruler, scissor parts, and fabric squares on the bulletin board. Fuse the spool, fabric triangle, and sewing-machine panels on the sewing machine.

5. Stitch around the larger shapes using a machine blanket stitch and the smaller shapes using a straight stitch to secure the edges.

6. Hand embroider the heart and thread using a stem stitch and 12-weight thread or two strands of embroidery floss. Embroider the needle using a backstitch. Refer to "Embroidery Stitches" on page 138 for stitching details.

7. Press the block on the wrong side and trim it to 6½" square, keeping the design centered.

Hashtag Love

• JANE DAVIDSON •

Social media has allowed the quilts and quilters of the world to enter our lives from all around the globe. Searching different social media platforms provides endless inspiration from the borderless quilting community. #Loveeverythingaboutquilting ~Jane

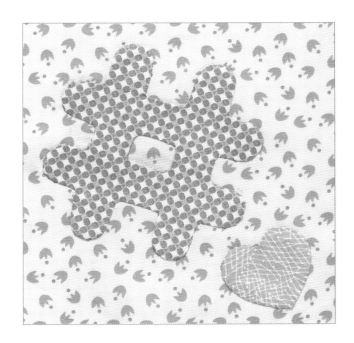

What You'll Need

1 cream print square, 7" × 7", for background

1 blue print square, 5" × 5", for hashtag

1 yellow print square, 3" × 3", for heart

Template plastic or freezer paper

Appliqué

The instructions are written for needle-turn appliqué.

1. Make templates from plastic or freezer paper using the patterns at right.

2. Prepare the appliqué pieces by tracing around the templates on the right side of the chosen fabrics. Cut out, adding a scant ¼" seam allowance all around.

3. Referring to the photo, position the hashtag and heart on the background square and appliqué in place.

4. Press the block on the wrong side and trim it to 6½" square, keeping the design centered.

Heart

Hashtag

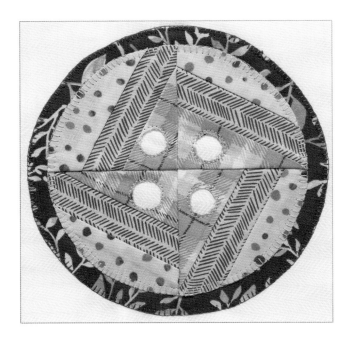

Button Up!

• CECILE MCPEAK & RACHEL MARTIN •

Our ultimate delight in quilting is to embellish with buttons. As a mother and daughter team, we enjoy working together to create the perfect button for every project. With Cecile leading the manufacturing and Rachel designing, we make a wondrous assortment of hand-dyed and handmade buttons to add texture and details to your quilted projects. ~Cecile and Rachel

What You'll Need

A: 1 cream print square, 7" × 7", for background

B: 1 navy print square, 7" × 7", for button rim

C: 1 blue plaid strip, 2" × 18", for button center

D: 1 blue print strip, 1¼" × 18", for button center

E: 1 blue dot strip, 2" × 18", for button center

Lightweight fusible web, 7" × 14"

Template plastic

Assembly

Press all seam allowances in the direction indicated by the arrows. The appliqué patterns are on pattern sheet 3. The instructions are written for fusible appliqué. If you prefer hand appliqué, reverse the patterns and add a seam allowance.

1. Join the C, D, and E strips. Press.

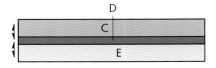

2. Make a plastic template using the square pattern, including the diagonal lines.

3. Place the template on the strip set, aligning the diagonal lines with the seams. Use a rotary cutter to cut around the template. Make four units that measure 3" square.

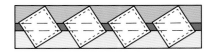

4. Join the units, making sure the same fabric meets at the center. The unit should measure 5½" square.

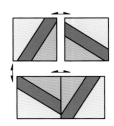

5. Trace the button rim and center patterns onto the fusible web, leaving ½" between shapes. Cut out the shapes, leaving about ¼" outside the lines.

6. Fuse the button rim to the wrong side of the B square. Center and fuse the button center to the wrong side of the unit from step 4. Cut out the shapes on the drawn lines.

7. Peel the paper backing from the button center and fuse it to the right side of the rim. Working from the wrong side of the rim, carefully cut out the buttonholes, cutting through all layers.

8. Peel away the paper backing from the button rim and fuse it in the center of the A square.

9. Stitch around the shapes with a machine blanket stitch to secure the edges. Press on the wrong side and trim to 6½" square.

Simply Bliss

• ROBIN VIZZONE •

Every time I enter my quilt studio, my heart feels happy. There are days when I know just walking through that doorway will bring me bliss, that's how much I enjoy creating. Quilting is truly in my heart, and hand sewing is my joy. If only I could find a way to attach some pins to my head, that would be true convenience! ~Robin

What You'll Need

A: 1 beige print square, 7" × 7", for background

B: 4 red print squares, 1½" × 1½", for body

C: 4 white print squares, 1½" × 1½", for body

D: 4 blue print squares, 1½" × 1½", for body

E: 1 white solid rectangle, 2½" × 3½", for head*

Freezer paper

12-weight cotton thread or embroidery floss: black

*For easier embroidery, start with a larger piece of white fabric.

Assembly and Appliqué

Press all seam allowances in the direction indicated by the arrows. For embroidery techniques and stitch detail, refer to "Embroidery Basics" on page 138. Robin hand pieced her block for a rustic appearance.

1. Arrange the squares in four rows of three squares each. When you are pleased with the arrangement, join the squares to make a 3½" × 4½" unit. Press.

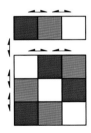

2. Using the pattern on pattern sheet 4, trace the head and body onto the dull side of freezer paper. Cut out the shapes on the traced lines. Press the body template onto the right side of the pieced unit and the head template onto the right side of the E rectangle. Trace around the templates. Cut out the body, adding a ¼" seam allowance. Remove the freezer-paper templates.

3. Using a light box or window, trace the eyes, nose, and mouth onto the head shape. Embroider the facial details using 12-weight thread, a backstitch, and running stitch. When embroidery is complete, cut out the head, adding a ¼" seam allowance.

4. Position the body and head on the background square, referring to the photo for placement and keeping an extra ½" around the outer edges. Stitch the appliqués by hand using a blind stitch.

5. Embroider the hairpins, arms, thread, needle, and button using 12-weight thread and a backstitch. Stitch four French knots in the center of the button.

6. Press the block on the wrong side and trim it to 6½" square, keeping the design centered.

Pack Your Bags

• JODIE CARLETON •

Way back in 2007, I started a craft blog, and years later I took my first overseas trip to attend Quilt Market in America. This block represents the crazy, sometimes misguided, but always fun adventure I find myself on in the world of quilting. ~Jodie

What You'll Need

A: 1 cream solid rectangle, 2½" × 3½"

1 red print square, 6" × 6"; cut into:

    B: 1 rectangle, 1" × 2½"

    C: 1 rectangle, 1½" × 2½"

    D: 2 rectangles, 1" × 5"

1 gray print piece, 7" × 8"; cut into:

    E: 2 squares, 1" × 1"

    F: 2 rectangles, 1¼" × 3½"

    G: 2 rectangles, 2" × 6½"

Embroidery floss: blue, tan

Assembly

Press all seam allowances in the direction indicated by the arrows. The embroidery pattern is on pattern sheet 2. For embroidery techniques and stitch detail, refer to "Embroidery Basics" on page 138.

1. Draw a diagonal line from corner to corner on the wrong side of the E squares. Referring to "Stitch and Flip" on page 137, place an E square on one end of each D rectangle as shown, noting the direction of the diagonal lines. Sew, trim, and press.

Make 1 of each.

2. Sew the units and the A, B, and C rectangles together as shown to make the block center. Press. The unit should measure 3½" × 5".

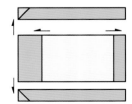

3. Sew the F rectangles to the sides of the block center. Sew the G rectangles to the top and bottom of the block. The block should measure 6½" square. Press.

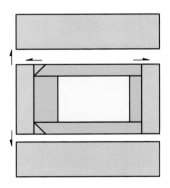

4. Embroider the string and word using a backstitch and four strands of embroidery floss. Use a French knot for the dot in *Quilt*.

Gran's Legacy

• NIKKI TERVO •

I learned everything to do with crafting from my beloved grandmother. She helped launch my design business and bought my first sewing machine so I could quilt. Her love was never-ending. She adored tea, brewed in a proper teapot. I think about her every day; without her I would never have shared so many cups of tea with my quilting friends. ~Nikki

What You'll Need

1 cream print square, 6" × 6"

2 different print strips, 1" × 5½"

2 different print strips, 1" × 6½"

1 lightweight fusible interfacing square, 6" × 6"

Embroidery floss: navy, blue green, red, gray

Basic embroidery supplies (page 138)

Embroidering the Block

Press all seam allowances in the direction indicated by the arrows. The embroidery pattern is on pattern sheet 1. For embroidery techniques and stitch detail, refer to "Embroidery Basics" on page 138.

1. Using a light box or window, trace the pattern onto the cream print square.

2. Fuse the square of interfacing to the wrong side of the cream square.

3. Embroider the design using two strands of embroidery floss. Use backstitches, running stitches, lazy daisies, and French knots.

4. Press the block on the wrong side and trim it to 5½" square, keeping the design centered.

EMBROIDERY FLOSS

Use one strand of embroidery floss for the letters if you prefer a finer look to the writing.

5. Sew the print 1" × 5½" strips to the top and bottom of the embroidered block and press. Sew the print 1" × 6½" strips to the sides of the block. Press.

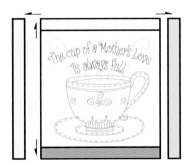

Cuppa

• PAT SLOAN •

Pouring a mug of coffee or brewing a pot of tea is a way that I slow down. I love the whole ritual of selecting a mug, watching the pot brew, and pouring the drink. Settling in with that warm mug and either some hand stitching or quilt books and magazines is a joy. This creates a little oasis in a busy day, and a warm mug in my hand signals it's break time. ~Pat

What You'll Need

1 tan check square, 7" × 7", for background

1 navy print square, 5" × 5", for cup and handle

1 red print square, 3" × 3", for heart

1 white print piece, 2" × 5", for trim

1 green print piece, 2" × 6", for saucer

Lightweight fusible web, 7" × 7"

12-weight cotton thread or embroidery floss: navy

Appliqué

The appliqué patterns are on pattern sheet 3. Instructions are written for fusible appliqué. If you prefer hand appliqué, reverse the patterns and add a seam allowance. For embroidery techniques and stitch detail, refer to "Embroidery Basics" on page 138.

1. Trace the patterns onto the fusible web, leaving ½" between the shapes. Cut out the shapes, leaving about ¼" outside the drawn lines. Cut out the interior of the cup and saucer, leaving ¼" of fusible web inside the drawn lines.

2. Fuse the shapes to the wrong side of the chosen fabrics, following the manufacturer's instructions. Cut out the shapes on the drawn lines and peel away the paper backing.

3. Position the cup and saucer. Tuck the handle under the edge of the cup. Position the trim on the cup and the heart above the cup. Fuse in place.

Appliqué placement guide

4. Stitch around the shapes with a machine blanket stitch to secure the edges of the appliqués.

5. Hand embroider the design using one strand of 12-weight thread or two strands of embroidery floss. Use a stem stitch for the solid lines and French knots for the dots.

6. Press the block on the wrong side and trim it to 6½" square, keeping the design centered.

Precious Things

• PATRINA JAHNKE •

This block represents the friendship that's at the heart of our community. Quilting brings people together and allows them to share a part of themselves in the quilts they create. The different fabrics represent the journeys we take and the people who come into our lives. ~Patrina

What You'll Need

1 cream print square, 4½" × 4½", for piece 1

Assorted scraps:

    12 rectangles, 2" × 6", for pieces 2–13

    4 rectangles, 2" × 4", for pieces 14–17

1 pink print square, 3" × 3", for heart

Lightweight fusible web, 3" × 3"

Paper for foundation piecing

Assembly and Appliqué

The instructions are written for fusible appliqué. The pattern is symmetrical and does not need to be reversed for hand appliqué. If you prefer hand appliqué, add a seam allowance.

1. Make one copy of the foundation pattern on pattern sheet 3.

2. Referring to "Foundation Piecing" on page 136, piece the block in numerical order, beginning with the cream square for piece 1. Trim and press each seam as a new piece is added.

3. When all the pieces have been added, press the block and trim to 6½" square. Carefully remove the foundation paper and press again.

4. Trace the heart pattern on pattern sheet 3 onto the fusible web. Cut out the shape, leaving about ¼" outside the drawn lines.

5. Fuse the shape to the wrong side of the pink print, following the manufacturer's instructions. Cut out the heart on the drawn lines and peel away the paper backing.

6. Fuse the heart in the center of the block. Stitch around the shape using a machine blanket stitch to secure the edges.

Little Things

• DAWN HEESE •

Time can be fleeting in our hurried world. I make it a point to relish the little things we are blessed with each day, whether it's a quiet moment on the deck stitching or watching my dog joyfully roll in the sunshine. ~Dawn

What You'll Need

1 gray print square, 7" × 7", for background

1 navy print square, 4½" × 4½", for cup and handle

1 blue print rectangle, 1" × 3", for trim

1 red print rectangle, 4" × 6", for hearts

1 green print square, 4" × 4", for leaves

Template plastic or freezer paper

Embroidery floss: green

Appliqué

The appliqué patterns are on pattern sheet 1. The instructions are written for needle-turn appliqué. Reverse the patterns for fusible appliqué. For embroidery techniques and stitch detail, refer to "Embroidery Basics" on page 138.

1. Make templates from plastic or freezer paper using the patterns.

2. Prepare the appliqué pieces by tracing around the templates onto the right side of the chosen fabrics. Cut out, adding a ¼" seam allowance all around.

3. Referring to the photo, position the shapes on the gray square, keeping ½" around the square's outer edges free from appliqué. Pin or baste in place. Stitch by hand using a blind stitch.

4. Embroider the stems using two strands of embroidery floss and a stem stitch.

5. Press the block on the wrong side and trim it to 6½" square, keeping the design centered.

MEASURE CAREFULLY

To prevent mistakes, measure your fabric carefully before you cut. It's simple, but so important! No one wants to waste fabric.

Balance

• WENCHE WOLFF HATLING •

It's all about finding balance in your life; balance between time for others and time for yourself. Sometimes I feel like my vintage toy where I'm trying to fit all of my life into a tiny spot. It's time to breathe—and let your feet find safe ground. ~Wenche

What You'll Need

1 light print square, 7" × 7" for background

1 gray print square, 6" × 6", for elephant

Scraps of red and navy prints for platform

Embroidery floss: blue, black

Template plastic or freezer paper

Appliqué

The appliqué patterns are on pattern sheet 3. The instructions are written for hand appliqué. Reverse the patterns for fusible appliqué.

1. Make templates from plastic or freezer paper using the patterns.

2. Prepare the appliqué pieces by tracing around the templates onto the right side of the chosen fabrics. Cut out, adding a ¼" seam allowance all around.

3. Referring to the photo, position the pieces in the center of the light print square and pin or baste in place. Stitch by hand using a blind stitch.

4. Embroider the eye using two strands of black embroidery floss and French knot. Embroider the head and ear using two strands of blue embroidery floss and backstitches. Embroider the tail using two strands of blue embroidery floss and two rows of backstitches. See "Embroidery Stitches" on page 138 for stitching details.

5. Press the block on the wrong side and trim it to 6½" square, keeping the design centered.

Cat Nap

• NICOLE VOS VAN AVEZATHE •

I got the idea for this embroidered quilt block when I saw my cat napping on a pile of quilts. One of the things I love about quilts is that they bring comfort and coziness to the whole family, furry family members included! ~Nicole

What You'll Need

1 light print square, 7" × 7", for background

Scraps of assorted prints for appliquéd blocks

Lightweight fusible web, 4" × 10"

Embroidery floss: green, brown, ecru, blue, red

Basic embroidery supplies (page 138)

Embroidery and Appliqué

For embroidery techniques and stitch detail, refer to "Embroidery Basics" on page 138. The appliqué patterns are on page 99. The instructions are written for fusible appliqué. If you prefer hand appliqué, reverse the patterns and add a seam allowance.

1. Using a light box or window, trace the embroidery pattern on pattern sheet 2 onto the light print square.

2. Embroider the design using one strand of embroidery floss and a stem stitch to outline the cat. Use backstitches for the eyes and straight stitches for the nose, whiskers, and paws. Use two strands and a running stitch for the grid, crosses, and petals. When stitching the crosses and petals, keep the stitching at least ½" from the outer edges.

PERFECT RUNNING STITCH

The best and fastest way to make a straight, even running stitch is to use a "sewing" method instead of a "stabbing" method. The sewing method means you're embroidering several stitches at once by entering the fabric with your needle, coming up again and repeating this a few times without pulling the needle and thread all the way through the fabric. A longer needle, such as a milliner's needle, is especially handy for this method. I find it easier to *not* use a hoop when stitching the running stitch. Hoop-less is definitely not hopeless! A hoop easily distorts fabric and your transferred straight lines may end up wobbly when embroidered. If you have transferred the grid correctly, your lines will be straight, and not using a hoop will make handling the fabric easier, too.

3. Trace the appliqué patterns onto the fusible web, leaving ½" between the shapes. Cut out the shapes, leaving about ¼" outside the drawn lines.

4. Fuse the shapes to the wrong side of the chosen fabrics, following the manufacturer's instructions. Cut out the shapes on the drawn lines and peel away the paper backing.

5. Referring to the photo, position the pieces on the block background. Fuse in place.

6. Stitch around the shapes using a hand blanket stitch and two strands of embroidery floss. You don't need to stitch any side that will be in the seam allowances.

7. Press the block on the wrong side and trim it to 6½" square, keeping the design centered.

ALTERNATE COLORWAY

Corner
Cut 1.

Bottom
Cut 1.

Side
Cut 1.

Patterns do not include seam allowances and are reversed for fusible appliqué.

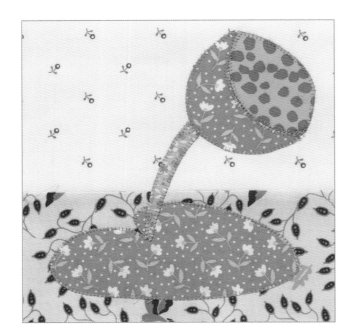

Lotus on Pond

• FIONA WRIGHT •

From my living room, I look out through low windows straight onto the fish pond. It's a peaceful and serene view with many goldfish, water lilies, and lotus. Perfect for contemplating a quilt design or the day ahead while enjoying a cup of tea. ~Fiona

What You'll Need

A: 1 cream print rectangle, 4" × 6½", for sky

B: 1 blue print rectangle, 3" × 6½", for pond

1 green print rectangle, 3" × 9", for lily pad and flower

1 yellow print rectangle, 1" × 3", for stem

1 olive-green dot square, 3" × 3", for flower center

Lightweight fusible web, 3" × 12"

Assembly and Appliqué

Press all seam allowances in the direction indicated by the arrows. The appliqué patterns are on pattern sheet 3. The instructions are written for fusible appliqué. If you prefer hand appliqué, reverse the patterns and add a seam allowance.

1. Sew the A and B rectangles together to make a 6½" block. Press.

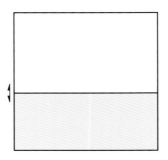

2. Trace the patterns onto the fusible web, leaving ½" between the shapes. Cut out the shapes, leaving about ¼" outside the drawn lines.

3. Fuse the shapes to the wrong side of the chosen fabrics, following the manufacturer's instructions. Cut out the shapes on the drawn lines and peel away the paper backing.

4. Referring to the photo, position the pieces on the block. Fuse the appliqués in place.

5. Stitch around the shapes with a machine blanket stitch to secure the edges. Press the block on the wrong side and trim it to 6½" square, keeping the design centered.

APPLIQUÉ STITCHES

For fusible appliqué, Pat generally uses a blanket stitch. On small pieces she switches to a straight stitch along the edge and a matching thread color.

Milk and Cookies

• REBECCA BRYAN •

Do I love milk and cookies? No! You can take the milk—I'll take the cookies! Just like my desserts, in my quilts I love simple pleasures like repeating shapes and secondary patterns. They go hand in hand, kind of like milk and cookies. Basic, but always scrumptious and satisfying. ~Rebecca

What You'll Need

A: 2 blue stripe squares,
   3⅞" × 3⅞"

B: 2 navy stripe squares,
   3⅞" × 3⅞"

C: 6 yellow print squares,
   2½" × 2½"

D: 6 green print squares,
   2½" × 2½"

1 red print square, 3½" × 3½"

Template plastic or freezer paper

Appliqué glue

Assembly and Appliqué

Press all seam allowances in the direction indicated by the arrows. The appliqué and wedge patterns are on pattern sheet 2. The instructions are written for needle-turn appliqué.

1. Draw a diagonal line from corner to corner on the wrong side of the A squares.

2. Referring to "Triangle Squares" on page 137, place an A square on a B square with right sides together. Sew, cut, and press to make two half-square-triangle units. Make four units that measure 3½" square.

Make 4.

3. Arrange and sew the four units together to make the block background that measures 6½" square.

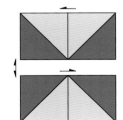

4. Make a template using the wedge pattern and template plastic or freezer paper. Trace the template onto the wrong side of each C and D square. Cut out along the lines to make six C wedges and six D wedges.

5. Sew the wedges together into pairs. Join the pairs to make a ring.

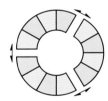

6. Use the seam lines to center the ring on the pieced background and glue or pin in place. Stitch around the outer edges by hand using a blind stitch.

7. Prepare the circle appliqué for your preferred method. Position the circle in the center of the ring. Using matching thread, appliqué it in place.

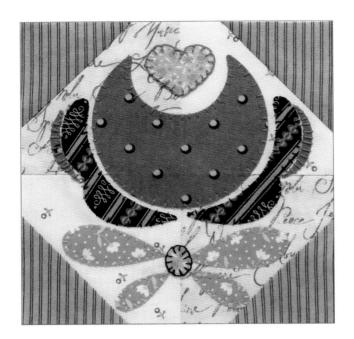

Flower Child

• CAROLEE MCMULLIN •

My kids call me Flower Child. It's a fitting nickname for me, and not only because I grew up in the '60s and '70s. My mother was an amazing homemaker, and she sewed almost all of our clothes. One Christmas she gave each of us a beautiful quilt made from our childhood clothing. I still have that quilt today and I cherish it. Scrappy quilts bring comfort to my soul and joy to my heart. ~Carolee

What You'll Need

A: 2 cream print squares, 3½" × 3½", for background

B: 2 beige print squares, 3½" × 3½", for background

C: 4 blue stripe squares, 2½" × 2½", for corner triangles

Scraps of assorted red, blue, yellow, and green prints for appliqué

Lightweight fusible web, 9" × 9"

Assembly and Appliqué

Press all seam allowances in the direction indicated by the arrows. The appliqué patterns are on pattern sheet 3. The instructions are written for fusible appliqué. The patterns are symmetrical and do not need to be reversed if you prefer to use hand appliqué.

1. Alternating the A and B squares, sew them together to make a Four Patch block that measures 6½" square. Press.

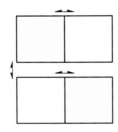

2. Draw a diagonal line from corner to corner on the wrong side of the C squares. Referring to "Stitch and Flip" on page 137, place a marked square on each corner of the block. Sew, trim, and press. **Note:** If using a striped fabric, place all squares with stripes running horizontally. Once sewn and pressed open, the stripes will be vertical.

3. Trace the patterns onto the fusible web, leaving ½" between the shapes. Cut out the shapes, leaving about ¼" outside the drawn lines. Fuse the shapes to the wrong side of the chosen fabrics, following the manufacturer's instructions. Cut out the shapes on the drawn lines and peel away the paper backing.

4. Referring to the photo, position the pieces on the block. Fuse the appliqués in place.

5. Stitch around the shapes using a hand or machine blanket stitch to secure the edges. Press the block on the wrong side.

Figure 8

• JANE DAVIDSON •

One of my favorite quilting motifs is the figure-eight pattern. There's nothing like the feel of guiding the sewing machine in a continual motion like an ice skater over the ice. ~Jane

What You'll Need

2 assorted dark print strips,
   3½" × 8"

2 assorted light print strips,
   3½" × 8"

4 squares, 4" × 4", of assorted
   prints for petals

Template plastic or freezer paper

Appliqué glue

Assembly

Press all seam allowances in the direction indicated by the arrows. The instructions are written for needle-turn appliqué. The patterns are symmetrical and do not need to be reversed if you prefer to use fusible appliqué.

1. Make a plastic template using the A and B patterns on pattern sheet 1. Trace the A template onto the wrong side of each of the four light and dark strips. Trace one B and one B reversed template onto the wrong side of each strip. Cut out the A and B triangles.

2. Sew a matching pair of B and B reversed triangles to each A triangle to make four units that measure 3½" square.

3. Arrange and sew the pieced units in two rows as shown. Press. Sew the rows together to make a 6½" block. Press.

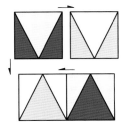

4. Use the petal pattern on pattern sheet 1 to make a plastic or freezer-paper template.

5. Prepare the appliqué pieces by tracing around the template on the right side of the chosen fabrics. Cut out, adding a scant ¼" seam allowance all around.

6. Using the photo as a guide, position the petals on the block. Pin or glue them in place. Stitch the appliqué shapes by hand using an appliqué stitch (page 135).

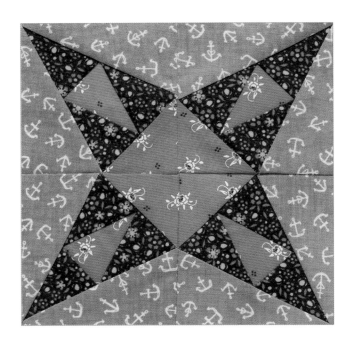

Iowa Star

• JODY SANDERS •

I started foundation piecing after taking a class from Carol Doak at Country Threads Quilt Shop in Garner, Iowa, in the early 1990s. I love how I get precise points using this technique. My pride in my home state of Iowa led me to draft a 6"-square pattern for the Iowa Star block. ~Jody

What You'll Need

1 red print piece, 7" × 9"; cut into
  4 rectangles, 2" × 2½", for piece 1
  2 squares, 3" × 3"; cut in half diagonally to make 4 triangles for piece 7
12 blue print rectangles, 2"x 2½", for pieces 2–4
8 gray print rectangles, 4" × 4½", for pieces 5 and 6
Paper for foundation piecing

Assembly

Press all seam allowances in the direction indicated by the arrows. Refer to "Foundation Piecing" on page 136 as needed.

1. Make four copies of the foundation pattern at right.

2. Piece each pattern in numerical order, beginning with the red rectangle for piece 1. Trim and press each seam as a new piece is added. Trim the pieced units along the outer lines, which includes a ¼" seam allowance.

3. Lay out the pieced units in two rows, rotating the units as shown. Sew the units into rows and press. Join the rows; press. Carefully remove the foundation papers and press again to make a 6½" block.

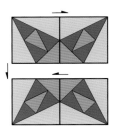

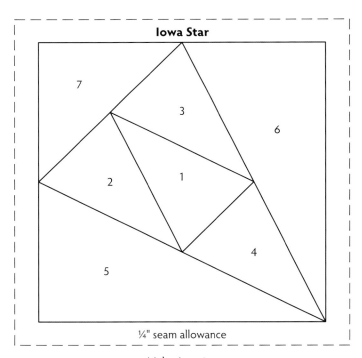

Iowa Star

¼" seam allowance

Make 4 copies.

Quilt Market

• ALEX VERONELLI •

Can you believe that until the year 2000, I had never heard the word quilt *before? These days my life is totally absorbed by the quilting world. I speak quilt, I eat quilt, I breathe quilt. ~Alex*

What You'll Need

14 assorted medium or dark print strips, 1¼" × 10" (collectively referred to as medium)*

7 assorted light prints, 1" × 10"

Alex used 2 strips each of red, green, yellow, blue, and brown prints and 4 strips of navy prints.

Assembly

Refer to the photo for fabric placement as needed. Press all seam allowances in the direction indicated by the arrows.

1. Sew a light strip between two medium strips to make section A and press. Trim the section to 2½" square.

2. Sew a light strip between two medium strips to make section B and press. Trim the section to 2½" × 4½".

3. Sew a light strip between two medium strips to make section C and press. Trim the section to 2½" × 6½". Make four sections.

4. Sew a light strip between two medium strips to make section D and press. Trim the section to 2½" × 8½".

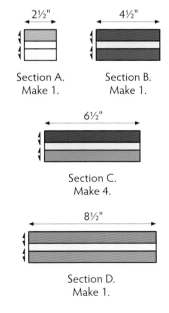

2½"

Section A.
Make 1.

4½"

Section B.
Make 1.

6½"

Section C.
Make 4.

8½"

Section D.
Make 1.

5. Arrange and sew sections A–D together as shown and press.

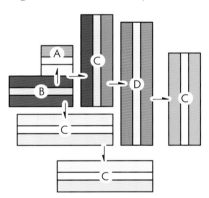

6. Use a rotary cutter and square ruler to trim the block to measure 6½" square.

Grandfather Clock

• KERRY GOULDER •

Time is fleeting. As a quilter, I'm easily swept away sewing or designing new ideas, without realizing how much time has passed. I designed Grandfather Clock as my way of remembering to always make time for my family, and to make every stitch count. ~Kerry

What You'll Need

1 tan herringbone square, 10" × 10"; cut into:
  1 rectangle, 1½" × 5", for A1
  1 rectangle, 2¾" × 4¼", for F
  1 rectangle, 1½" × 4", for G1
  2 rectangles, 1½" × 2½", for H5 and H6
  2 rectangles, 1½" × 2½", for I1 and J1

1 tan floral piece, 10" × 12"; cut into:
  2 rectangles, 1" × 2", for A2 and A3
  3 rectangles, 1½" × 2½", for A4, I2, and J2
  3 rectangles, 1½" × 3", for A5, B4, and C4
  2 rectangles, 2" × 3", for A6 and A9
  2 squares, 1" × 1", for B1 and C1
  2 rectangles, 1½" × 5½", for D2 and E2
  1 rectangle, 1½" × 7", for K1

1 white solid square, 12" × 12"; cut into:
  2 squares, 1" × 1", for B2 and C2
  2 rectangles, 1½" × 2", for B3 and C3
  2 rectangles, 1½" × 5½", for D1 and E1
  6 rectangles, 1½" × 2½", for A7, A8, A10, A11, K2, and K3
  1 square, 4" × 4", for clock face

1 navy print piece, 6" × 7"; cut into:
  2 rectangles, 1" × 2", for G2 and G4
  4 rectangles, 1½" × 2½", for G3, G5, H2, and H3
  1 rectangle, 2" × 4", for H4

1 blue print square, 5" × 5"; cut into:
  1 rectangle, 1" × 1½", for H1
  1 square, 2" × 2", for pendulum
  1 square, 1" × 1", for clock dial

1 red print square, 5" × 5", for clock face rim

Lightweight fusible stabilizer, 4" × 4"
Embroidery floss: navy
Water-soluble pen
Paper for foundation piecing
Template plastic or freezer paper
Water-soluble marker

Assembly and Appliqué

Press all seam allowances in the direction indicated by the arrows. Refer to "Foundation Piecing" on page 136 as needed. The foundation-piecing patterns and appliqué patterns are on pattern sheet 4. The instructions are written for hand appliqué. The appliqué patterns are symmetrical and do not need to be reversed if you prefer to use fusible appliqué.

1. Make one copy of each foundation pattern A–K.

2. Sew each section in numerical order, starting with section A. Trim and press each seam as a new piece is added.

3. Trim each section on the outer lines, which includes a ¼" seam allowance.

4. Stitch sections A, B, and C together and press.

5. Stitch sections G, H, I, and J together and press. Add the F rectangle; press.

6. Stitch sections D and E to the unit from step 5. Press.

7. Join the sections as shown and press.

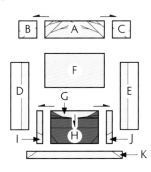

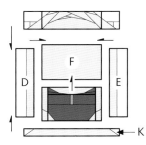

8. Use a water-soluble marker to draw guidelines on the F and H pieces for the appliqué placement as indicated on the foundation paper.

9. Make templates from plastic or freezer paper using the clock face rim, clock face, pendulum, and dial patterns.

10. Prepare the appliqué pieces by tracing around the templates on the right side of the selected fabrics. Cut out all pieces except the clock face, adding a scant ¼" seam allowance all around.

11. Transfer the clock face embroidery to the white fabric. Use the clock face template to cut one clock face from the stabilizer. Fuse the stabilizer in the center of the white clock face piece. Embroider the clock face

using two strands of embroidery floss and the backstitch. See "Embroidery Stitches" on page 138 for stitching instructions.

12. Cut out the clock face, adding a scant ¼" seam allowance. Position the appliqué shapes on the clock. Pin or baste the shapes in place and hand appliqué them using a blind stitch (page 135). Press from the wrong side to make a 6½" block.

ALTERNATE COLORWAY

Curves Forever

• JENNY PEDIGO & HELEN ROBINSON •

Our block represents our LOVE of curves. We adore the motion that curves bring to quilt designs and feel curves are the perfect complement to any quilt! ~Jenny and Helen

What You'll Need

2 blue print squares, 5" × 5"

2 red stripe squares, 5" × 5"

4 cream plaid squares, 3¼" × 3¼"

Template plastic

Preparation and Assembly

Press all seam allowances in the direction indicated by the arrows.

1. Make a template for pieces A, C, and D using the patterns on pattern sheet 3 and the template plastic.

2. Stack the blue and red squares right side facing up and raw edges aligned. Position the A template on the stack with the corner and raw edges aligned. Using a rotary cutter, carefully cut along the curved edge of the template to create shapes A and B.

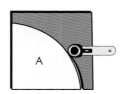

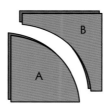

3. Stack the cream squares right side facing up and raw edges aligned. Position the C template on the stack with the corner and raw edges aligned. Using a rotary cutter, carefully cut along the curved edge of the template to create shape C. Discard the small piece.

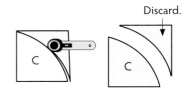

4. Position A on B, right sides together, with a ½" of B extending beyond A. Sew slowly, aligning the curved edges as you sew. Press. Make two of each unit.

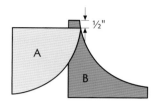

Make 2 of each.

5. Position the D template on the A corner of each unit as shown. Using a rotary cutter, carefully cut along the curved edge. Discard the small piece.

Discard.

6. Position a C piece on each unit from step 2, right sides together, with a ¼" of C extending beyond the unit as shown. Sew slowly and align the curved edges as you sew. Press. Make two of each unit.

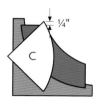

Make 2 of each.

7. Position a ruler on each unit, with the 3½" marks on the ruler aligned with the curved seam as shown. Trim two sides. Rotate the unit 180°, align the 3½" marks on the ruler with the newly cut edges. Trim the excess fabric. Repeat to trim all of the units.

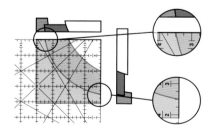

8. Arrange and sew the pieced units in rows as shown. Press. Sew the rows together; press. The block should measure 6½" square.

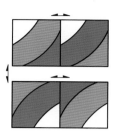

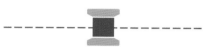

JOIN THE FUN

Never feel like you're falling behind when making Splendid Sampler blocks. Instead, think of it as joining in when you please. It might be the same block others are making, or it might be the one that *you* want to stitch. Join in and sew with us, no matter where you start or how many blocks you make.

Stars Above

• CATH HALL •

My block is named for my obsession with quilted (and real) stars. No matter where I am in the world, I always look up at the stars and search for the familiar patterns of Australia's constellations—sometimes I see them, and sometimes I don't. ~Cath

What You'll Need

4 red print strips, 1¼" × 4", for piece 1

4 blue print strips, 1¼" × 4", for piece 2

8 navy print rectangles, 1¼" × 3", for sections 3 and 4

8 tan check squares, 4" × 4", for sections 5 and 6

Paper for foundation piecing

Assembly

Press all seam allowances in the direction indicated by the arrows. Refer to "Foundation Piecing" on page 136 as needed.

1. Make four copies of the foundation pattern on pattern sheet 3.

2. Piece the block units in numerical order. Trim and press each seam as a new piece is added.

3. When all the pieces have been added, trim each unit on the outer lines, which includes a ¼" seam allowance.

4. Leaving the paper in place, join the units as shown and press. Carefully remove the foundation paper and press again to make a 6½" block.

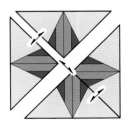

COLOR CODE THE PATTERNS

To prevent any confusion with fabric placement, I recommend using colored pencils or markers to mark each section of the pattern with the corresponding fabric color. This is a good way to check that you've placed the right fabric piece in the right spot.

Get to the Point

• RHONDA PIERCE •

The sewing-machine needle is neither glamorous nor sexy, but it's a sewing essential. Representing Schmetz needles allows me to contribute professionally to our sewing world. Yes, someone must remind you to change your needle! Every day I see the power of that little 2" piece of steel expressed in quilters' creative projects. ~Rhonda

What You'll Need

1 cream plaid piece, 6" × 8"; cut into:

    2 rectangles, 1½" × 3½", for A1 and A3

    1 square, 2½" × 2½"; cut in half diagonally to make 2 triangles for A4 and A5

    1 rectangle, 1¼" × 4", for A6

    1 square, 4" × 4", for B1

1 red stripe square, 10" × 10"; cut into:

    1 rectangle, 2" × 3½", for A2

    2 rectangles, 2¼" × 4", for A7 and A8

    2 rectangles, 4" × 5", for B2 and B3

Paper for foundation piecing

Assembly

Press all seam allowances in the direction indicated by the arrows. Refer to "Foundation Piecing" on page 136 as needed.

1. Make one copy each of foundation patterns A and B on pattern sheet 4.

2. Sew each section in numerical order, starting with section A. Trim and press each seam as a new piece is added.

3. Trim each section along the outer lines, which includes a ¼" seam allowance.

4. Join the sections as shown and press to make a 6½" block. Carefully remove the foundation paper and press again.

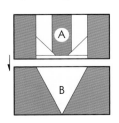

USING STRIPES

When using a directional print, such as a stripe, make an extra copy of the block patterns and then use a rotary cutter to cut out the piece on what would be the stitching line. Use these paper templates to "rough cut" the shapes, making sure to include at least a ¼" seam allowance on all sides of each template. That way your stripes are sure to be going in the correct direction.

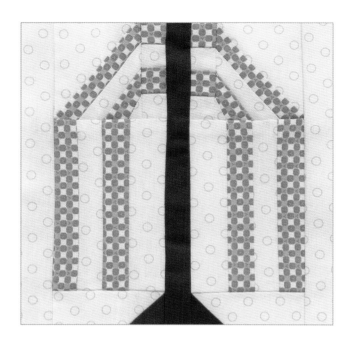

Happy Willow

• JENIFER GASTON •

Growing up, we traveled a lot to visit family. Dad would tell us to look for deer or count the cows to keep us from bickering. I counted weeping willow trees. And when I was 12, my parents planted one for me! I'm happiest designing projects related to nature. ~Jenifer

What You'll Need

1 cream print square, 10" × 10", for background; cut into:

2 strips, 1" × 6½"

2 strips, 1" × 4"

2 strips, 1¼" × 4"

2 strips, 1" × 3"

2 rectangles, 1" × 2¾"

2 rectangles, 2½" × 3", for A1 and B1

2 strips, 1" × 3½", for A3 and B3

2 squares, 1½" × 1½", for A5 and B5

1 green print square, 8" × 8"; cut into:

4 strips, 1" × 4", for branches

2 strips, 1" × 3", for branches

2 strips, 1" × 3¾", for A2 and B2

2 strips, 1" × 2½", for A4 and B4

1 brown solid strip, 2" × 9"; cut into:

1 strip, 1" × 6½", for tree trunk

2 squares, 1" × 1", for tree base

Paper for foundation piecing

Assembly

Press all seam allowances in the direction indicated by the arrows. Refer to "Foundation Piecing" on page 136 as needed.

1. Make one copy each of foundation patterns A and B on pattern sheet 4.

2. Piece the A pattern in numerical order, beginning with a cream rectangle for piece 1. Trim and press each seam as a new piece is added. Repeat to piece the B pattern.

3. When all the pieces have been added, press each unit and trim to 2¼" × 2½". Carefully remove the foundation paper and press again.

4. Join two cream and two green 1" × 3" strips to make a strip set. Press. Cut the strip set into two 1" × 2½" segments.

Make 1 strip set. Cut 2 segments.

5. Join a segment to the A and B units as shown and press.

Make 1 of each.

6. Sew a cream 1" × 4" strip between two green 1" × 4" strips and press. Add a cream 1¼" × 4" strip and press. Make two.

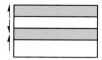

Make 2.

7. Referring to "Stitch and Flip" on page 137, draw a diagonal line from corner to corner on the wrong side of the brown 1" squares. Sew a marked square on one end of each cream 1" × 2¾" rectangle.

Make 1 of each.

8. Join the units from steps 5–7 as shown below to make left and right branch units. Press.

9. Sew the cream 1" × 6½" strips, brown 1" × 6½" strip, and the branch units from step 8 together to make a 6½" block. Press.

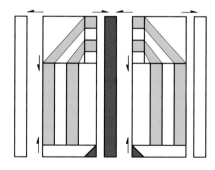

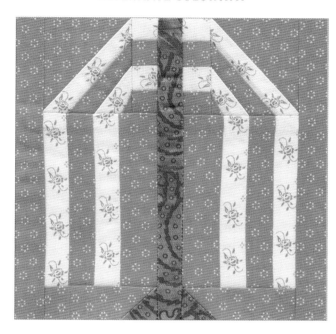

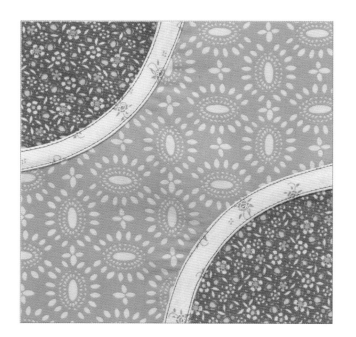

Mod Bowtie

• KRISTA HENNEBURY •

Traditional quilts and quilt blocks provide endless inspiration. I like to challenge myself to think of fun, simple ways to renew traditional designs, either through different construction methods, colors, or by altering scale. This bow-tie variation is constructed without any curved piecing! Finding shortcuts to achieve familiar results keeps me entertained and engaged in this work that I love. ~Krista

What You'll Need

A: 1 green print square, 6¾" × 6¾"

B: 2 red print squares, 4" × 4"

C: 2 cream print bias strips, 1½" × 6"

Template plastic or freezer paper

Appliqué glue or fabric glue stick

Appliqué and Assembly

1. Use the pattern on pattern sheet 2 and plastic or freezer paper to make a template. Use the template to cut a quarter circle from each B square.

2. On the wrong side, apply a thin line of glue to the curved edge of each quarter circle. Glue-baste the quarter circles to opposite diagonal corners of the A square, aligning the raw edges as shown.

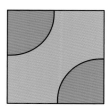

3. Press each C strip in half lengthwise, wrong sides together.

4. Apply a thin line of glue to the right side of the curved edge of each quarter circle. Glue-baste the bias strip in place, matching the raw edges of the strip to the curved edge of the quarter circles.

Sew the bias strip along the curve using a scant ¼" seam allowance.

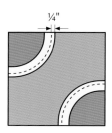

5. Press the folded edge of the strip toward the center of the block and pin in place. Topstitch both edges of the strip. Carefully trim away the A print from underneath the quarter circles, leaving ¼" for seam allowances.

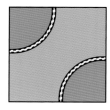

6. Press and trim the block to 6½" square, keeping the design centered.

Flowering Tree

• AMY FRIEND •

I often find inspiration while on morning walks on the back roads and trails in my town. Walking frees my mind, and nature is so beautiful it often leads me to creative ideas. ~Amy

What You'll Need

1 red print piece, 9" × 11"; cut into:

    2 rectangles, 2" × 3", for A1 and B1

    2 rectangles, 2" × 4", for A3 and B3

    4 rectangles, 2" × 5½", for A5, A7, B5, and B7

1 cream print square, 10" × 10"; cut into:

    2 rectangles, 1" × 3½", for A2 and B2

    4 rectangles, 1" × 4½", for A4, A6, B4, and B6

    2 strips, 1½" × 7", for A8 and B8

1 navy print piece, 6" × 11"; cut into:

    2 rectangles, 2½" × 4½", for A9 and B9

    2 rectangles, 3" × 5", for A10 and B10

Paper for foundation piecing

Assembly

Press all seam allowances in the direction indicated by the arrows. Refer to "Foundation Piecing" on page 136 as needed.

1. Make one copy of each foundation pattern on pattern sheet 3.

2. Sew each section in numerical order. Trim and press each seam as a new piece is added.

3. Trim each section on the outer lines, which includes a ¼" seam allowance.

4. Stitch section A to B and press. Carefully remove the foundation paper and press again to make a 6½" block.

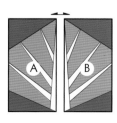

FOUNDATION PAPERS

You can remove the papers once the block is finished or leave them in your block until you've sewn the block into the quilt top. Paper-pieced blocks tend to have a lot of bias edges, and waiting to remove the papers will help avoid stretching, keeping the block nice and square.

Country Star

• NANCY MAHONEY •

After living in an urban environment for most of my life, I moved to a house in the country and came to truly appreciate the beauty of the night sky. I love seeing all the twinkling stars. Maybe that's why I like using Star blocks in many of my quilts. ~Nancy

What You'll Need

4 yellow print rectangles, 2" × 3", for A1

12 red print rectangles, 1¾" × 2½", for A2, A3, and B2

4 navy print rectangles, 2½" × 3", for A4

4 blue rectangles, 2" × 2¾", for B1

8 cream print #1 rectangles, 2¼" × 3½", for B3 and B4

4 green print rectangles, 1½" × 2½", for C1

8 cream print #2 rectangles, 1¾" × 3½", for C2 and C3

Paper for foundation piecing

Assembly

Press all seam allowances in the direction indicated by the arrows. Refer to "Foundation Piecing" on page 136 as needed.

1. Make four copies each of foundation patterns A–C on pattern sheet 3.

2. Piece each A pattern in numerical order, beginning with a yellow print for piece A1. Trim and press each seam as a new piece is added. After adding the last piece, trim around the unit along the outer lines, which allows for a ¼" seam allowance. Repeat the process for the B and C sections.

3. Stitch section B to C and press. Make 4.

Make 4.

4. Join the A and B/C sections in pairs. Press. Sew the pairs together to make a 6½" block. Press. Carefully remove the foundation paper and press again.

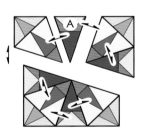

STAYING PUT

Instead of using a pin to hold the first piece of fabric in place on the paper, use a glue stick to apply a dab of glue. This way the paper lies flat when trimming and adding the second piece of fabric.

Star Plus

• CHERYL BRICKEY •

I'm at my quilting best after spending a day with my husband and two children. My family grounds me and recharges me. They are the stars of my life and the inspiration for this block design. ~Cheryl

What You'll Need

1 navy print piece, 6" × 9"; cut into:
   4 rectangles, 1½" × 2¾", for A1
   4 squares, 2¾" × 2¾", for B1

4 tan print rectangles, 1½" × 3½", for A2

1 red print square, 7" × 7"; cut into:
   4 rectangles, 1½" × 4", for A3
   2 rectangles, 1" × 1¼", for C
   1 rectangle, 1" × 2½", for E

2 cream print squares, 3½" × 3½"; cut in half diagonally to make 4 triangles for A4

1 blue print piece, 8" × 9"; cut into:
   8 rectangles, 1¾" × 3½", for B2 and B3
   4 squares, 1¼" × 1¼", for D

Paper for foundation piecing

Assembly

Press all seam allowances in the direction indicated by the arrows. Refer to "Foundation Piecing" on page 136 as needed.

1. Make four copies each of foundation patterns A and B on pattern sheet 2.

2. Piece each A pattern in numerical order, beginning with a navy print for piece A1. Trim and press each seam as a new piece is added. After adding the last piece, trim around the unit along the outer lines, which allows for a ¼" seam allowance.

3. Repeat the process for each B section.

4. Sew a C rectangle between two D squares and press. Make two and sew them to opposite sides of the E rectangle to make the block center that measures 2½" square. Press.

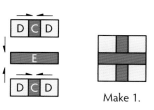

Make 1.

5. Arrange and sew the pieced units in rows as shown. Press. Sew the rows together. Press.

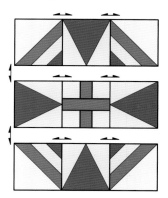

6. Carefully remove the foundation paper and press again to make a 6½" block.

My Own Little Corner

• SHANNON GILLMAN ORR •

Nothing's better than being tucked into my studio, door closed, headphones on, and singing while sewing. In my studio, I'm an adventurer, an artist who makes up her own rules. Quilting and making continually help me discover my best self.
~Shannon

What You'll Need

1 red print square, 7" × 7"; cut into:
- 1 square, 4½" × 4½", for A1
- 2 rectangles, 1¾" × 2¾", for B2 and B3
- 2 squares, 1½" × 1½", for C2 and C3

1 blue print rectangle, 1¾" × 2¾", for B1

1 tan print square, 4" × 4"; cut into:
- 1 rectangle, 1¼" × 2½", for C1
- 2 rectangles, 1¼" × 3¾", for A2 and D2

1 navy print square, 9" × 9"; cut into:
- 1 rectangle, 1" × 3½", for E
- 2 strips, 2" × 6½", for G and H
- 2 squares, 3½" × 3½", for D1 and F

1 green print square, 1¾" × 1¾", for hexagon

2 green felt squares, 1¾" × 1¾", for hexagons

1 cream print square, 1¾" × 1¾", for heart

Lightweight fusible web, 4" × 4"

Embroidery floss: pink

Paper for foundation piecing

Assembly

Press all seam allowances in the direction indicated by the arrows. Refer to "Foundation Piecing" on page 136 as needed.

1. Make one copy of each foundation pattern on page 119.

2. Sew each section A–D in numerical order, starting with section A. Trim and press each seam as a new piece is added.

3. Trim around each section along the outer lines, which allows for a ¼" seam allowance.

4. Stitch section A to B. Press. Sew section C to the bottom of A/B. Press. Add section D to the top of A/B. Press.

5. Stitch the E rectangle to the bottom of the house unit and press. Stitch the F square to the top to complete the house section. Press. Trim the section to 3½" × 6½".

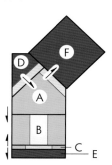

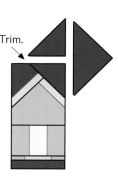

6. Sew the G and H strips to the sides of the house section to make a 6½" block. Press.

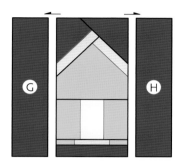

7. Using the patterns at right, trace the hexagon three times and the heart one time onto the fusible web, leaving ½" between the shapes. Cut out the shapes, leaving about ¼" outside the drawn lines.

8. Fuse the shapes to the wrong side of the chosen fabrics, following the manufacturer's instructions. Cut out the shapes on the drawn lines and peel away the paper backing.

9. Referring to the photo, position the pieces on the block and fuse them in place. Topstitch around the outer edges of each hexagon. Stitch around the outer edges of the heart using three strands of embroidery floss and a backstitch. See "Embroidery Stitches" on page 138 for stitching instructions.

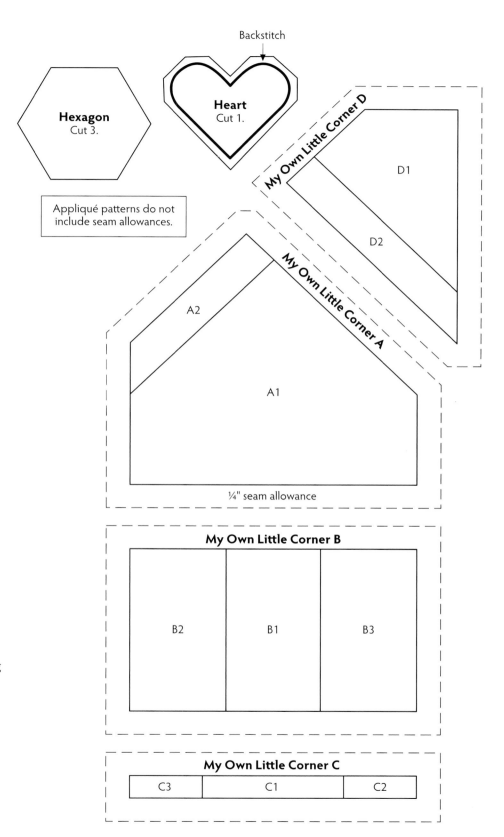

Winter Flower

• JODI GODFREY •

I designed this block during a spontaneous and chaotic interstate move in the middle of winter. As we drove into our new driveway after a huge day of packing the truck and driving hundreds of miles, the first thing I noticed were the flowering bulbs, planted by the previous owner. What a sweet surprise! I cut a bouquet and the beautiful fragrance filled my new studio. ~Jodi

What You'll Need

1 navy floral piece, 9" × 11", for A

1 yellow print piece, 7" × 11", for B and C

1 blue print piece, 9" × 12", for D

Template plastic

Cardstock for English-paper-piecing foundations

Assembly

Refer to "English Paper Piecing" on page 136 as needed.

1. Make a template for pieces A–D using the patterns on pattern sheet 2 and the template plastic. Trace the template onto the cardstock and cut out exactly on the line to make the foundations.

2. Pin the shapes to the fabrics specified below and cut out, adding a ⅜" seam allowance all around for basting.

- Navy floral: 8 of A

- Yellow print: 4 each of pieces B and C

- Blue print: 4 each of D and D reverse

3. Fold the fabric seam allowance over the foundations and baste through all thicknesses.

4. Sew two A pieces to each B piece, right sides together, using a whipstitch (page 136). Sew the A/B pieces together as shown to make the block center.

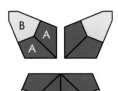

5. Sew a D and a D reverse triangle to each C piece to make four side units. Sew the side units to the block center.

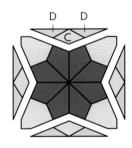

6. Clip the basting threads, remove the paper foundations, unfold the outer seam allowances, and press. Trim the block to 6½" square, leaving a ¼" seam allowance beyond the points of the C pieces.

Shared Squares

• JAMIE MUELLER & JILL RIMES •

We love quilting as a family. We're a mother/daughter duo and our best quilts are those we created together. Jamie grew up playing under quilt frames while Jill hand quilted. Sharing the love of quilting with others is our passion. ~Jamie and Jill

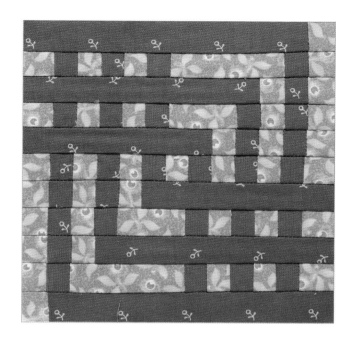

What You'll Need

1 red print piece, 9" × 15", cut into:

  2 rectangles, 1½" × 6½", for A1 and K2

  2 rectangles, 1½" × 5½", for C1 and I4

  2 rectangles, 1½" × 4½", for E1 and G6

  30 squares, 1½" × 1½", for B2, B4, B6, B8, C3, D2, D4, D6, D8, D10, E3, E5, F2, F4, F6, F8, F10, F12, G2, G4, H2, H4, H6, H8, H10, I2, J2, J4, J6, and J8

1 green print piece, 10" × 15", cut into:

  37 squares, 1½" × 1½", for A2, B1, B3, B5, B9, C2, C4, D1, D3, D5, D9, D11, E2, E4, E6, F1, F3, F5, F7, F9, F11, F13, G1, G3, G5, H1, H3, H7, H9, H11, I1, I3, J1, J5, J7, J9, and K1

  4 rectangles, 1½" × 4", for B7, D7, H5, and J3

Paper for foundation piecing

FABRIC SELECTION

High contrast between two fabrics is important for the design to show in this block.

Assembly

Press the seam allowances in the direction indicated by the arrows. Refer to "Foundation Piecing" on page 136 as needed.

1. Make one copy of each foundation pattern A–K on pattern sheet 4.

2. Sew each section in numerical order, starting with section A. Trim and press each seam as a new piece is added.

3. Trim each section on the outer lines, which includes a ¼" seam allowance.

4. Arrange the sections in alphabetical order, starting with section A. Join the sections and press to make a 6½" block. Carefully remove the foundation papers and press.

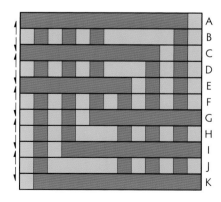

Adventure Abounds

• KITTY WILKIN •

Finding ways to intertwine quilting with my love of nature and outdoor adventuring with my family is my passion. I take quilt photographs in gorgeous natural places and make summer-adventure milestone quilts. Adventure abounds in life, so why not capture it in a quilt? ~Kitty

What You'll Need

1 cream solid piece, 10" × 14"; cut into:
- 2 squares, 1½" × 1½", for A1 and D2
- 1 rectangle, 2¼" × 2½", for A4
- 1 rectangle, 2¼" × 3¼", for A5
- 1 rectangle, 3" × 3½", for A6
- 2 rectangles, 2½" × 3", for B6 and F1
- 1 rectangle, 3" × 5", for A7
- 1 square, 2" × 2", for B2
- 5 rectangles, 1½" × 2¼", for B3, B4, D4, E2, and E3
- 1 rectangle, 2" × 3", for B7
- 2 rectangles, 1½" × 2", for C2 and C3
- 1 rectangle, 1¾" × 3", for F3
- 1 rectangle, 2¼" × 3", for F5
- 1 rectangle, 2¾" × 3", for F7

1 red print rectangle, 1½" × 4"; cut into:
- 1 square, 1½" × 1½", for A2
- 1 rectangle, 1½" × 2¼", for A3

1 dark green solid square, 4" × 4"; cut into:
- 1 rectangle, 1¼" × 1¾", for B1
- 1 rectangle, 1¾" × 3", for C1
- 1 square, 1½" × 1½", for D1

1 green print square, 4" × 4"; cut into:
- 1 rectangle, 1½" × 2¼", for B5
- 1 rectangle, 1¾" × 3½", for D3

1 brown print rectangle, 1" × 1¾", for E1

1 blue print #1 rectangle, 1¼" × 2½", for F2

1 blue print #2 rectangle, 1½" × 2¼", for F4

1 blue print #3 rectangle, 1¾" × 3", for F6

1 navy print rectangle, 2¼" × 4", for F8

Paper for foundation piecing

Assembly

Press seam allowances as indicated by the arrows. Refer to "Foundation Piecing" on page 136.

1. Make one copy of each foundation pattern A–F on pattern sheet 4.

2. Sew each section in numerical order, starting with section A. Trim and press each seam as a new piece is added.

3. Trim each section on the outer lines, which includes a ¼" seam allowance all around.

4. Join sections B–E to make the tree unit. Press.

5. Sew section A to the tree unit; press. Sew section F to the bottom of the unit to make a 6½" block; press. Carefully remove the foundation paper and press again.

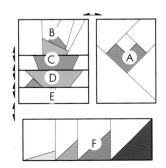

Betty's Bloom

• CARL HENTSCH •

I'm living my best quilting life when I'm sitting in front of my sewing machine or sharing good times with quilt friends over a glass of wine. I named this block Betty's Bloom after my oldest dog, who shares time with me on the sofa while I hand piece. ~Carl

What You'll Need

1 navy print square, 9" × 9";
  cut into:

  2 squares, 3" × 3"; cut in
    half diagonally to make 4
    triangles for A1

  4 rectangles, 2" × 4", for B2

8 cream print rectangles, 1" × 3",
  for A2 and B3

1 green print square, 9" × 9";
  cut into:

  4 rectangles, 2" × 4", for A3

  2 squares, 3" × 3"; cut in
    half diagonally to make 4
    triangles for B4

4 navy tone on tone rectangles,
  2½" × 4½", for A4

4 blue floral rectangles,
  2½" × 4½", for B1

2 red print squares, 1⅜" × 1⅜"; cut
  in half diagonally for C

Paper for foundation piecing

Assembly

Press all seam allowances in the direction indicated by the arrows. Refer to "Foundation Piecing" on page 136 as needed.

1. Make four copies each of foundation patterns A and B on pattern sheet 4.

2. Piece each A pattern in numerical order, beginning with a navy print for piece A1. Trim and press each seam as a new piece is added. After adding the last piece, trim around the unit along the outer lines, which includes a ¼" seam allowance.

3. Repeat the process for each B section.

4. Stitch section A to B and press. Sew a C triangle to each A/B unit and press. Make four block quarters.

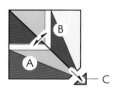

5. Lay out the block quarters and join them into rows and press. Join the rows; press to make a 6½" block. Carefully remove the foundation paper and press again.

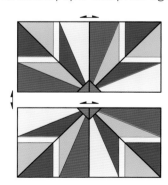

Split Hexie Flower

• NICOLE DAKSIEWICZ •

I started hand sewing while traveling for work. English paper piecing was a portable and fun way to stay busy and keep creative ideas flowing while away from my sewing machine. Pieced hexies are my favorite way to incorporate sewing at my machine and hand stitching. ~Nicole

What You'll Need

A: 1 navy print square, 7" × 7", for background

B: 1 blue print strip, 1½" × 19", for hexagons

C: 1 light print strip, 1½" × 19", for hexagons

Template plastic

Cardstock for English paper piecing

Assembly

Press all seam allowances in the direction indicated by the arrows. Refer to "English Paper Piecing" on page 136 as needed.

1. Sew the B and C strips together to make a strip set and press. Cut the strip set into six 3"-wide segments.

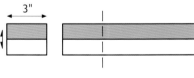

Make 1 strip set.
Cut 6 segments.

2. Make a template using the hexagon pattern on page 125 and the template plastic. Trace the template onto the cardstock and cut out directly on the line to make six foundations.

3. Pin a hexagon shape to the wrong side of each segment and cut out, adding a ⅜" seam allowance all around for basting. Be sure to keep the points of the hexagon aligned with the seamlines so the shape is centered.

4. Fold the fabric seam allowance over the foundations and baste through all thicknesses.

Baste.

Make 6.

5. Whipstitch (page 136) the six hexagons together to make the hexagon ring. Press and remove the basting stitches and papers.

6. Position the hexagon ring in the center of the A square and pin or glue-baste in place to create the flower. Stitch around the outer and inner edges of the flower using a machine blanket stitch and matching thread.

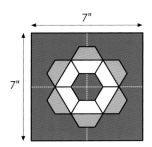

Appliqué placement guide

7. Press the block on the wrong side and trim it to 6½" square, keeping the design centered.

ALTERNATE COLORWAY

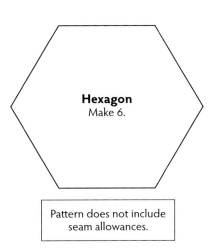

Hexagon
Make 6.

Pattern does not include
seam allowances.

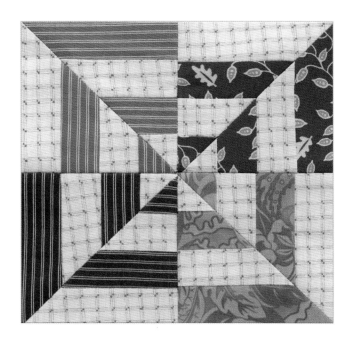

Ticker Tape

• DEBBY BROWN •

Before designing a quilt, I think first about how I'll quilt it. I designed this block with long, narrow strips that are perfect for ribbon candy quilting—my favorite machine-quilting pattern. I feel like partying each time I get to quilt a ribbon candy design! ~Debby

What You'll Need

1 cream print piece, 9" × 13"; cut into:
  4 rectangles, 2" × 4", for A1
  8 rectangles, 2" × 3", for A3 and B3
  4 squares, 2" × 2", for B1
4 assorted print rectangles, 5" × 7"; cut *each* into:
  2 rectangles, 2" × 3", for A2 and B2 (8 total)
  1 square, 2" × 2", for A4 (4 total)
  1 rectangle, 2" × 4", for B4 (4 total)
Paper for foundation piecing

Assembly

Press all seam allowances in the direction indicated by the arrows. Refer to "Foundation Piecing" on page 136 as needed.

1. Make four copies each of foundation patterns A and B on pattern sheet 3.

2. Piece each A pattern in numerical order, beginning with a cream print for piece A1. Trim and press each seam as a new piece is added. After adding the last piece, trim around the unit along the outer lines, which allows for a ¼" seam allowance.

3. Repeat the process for each B section.

4. Stitch section A to B and press. Make four block quarters.

Make 4.

5. Arrange and sew the block quarters into rows and press. Join the rows; press to make a 6½" block. Carefully remove the foundation paper and press again.

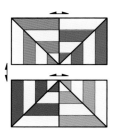

Connection

• SHERI CIFALDI-MORRILL •

My block is inspired by how I feel when the idea for a quilt comes together and the concept and design are connected. There's this wonderful spark when the layout, fabric selection, and quilting all support one another. ~Sheri

What You'll Need

6 red print rectangles, 1¼" × 2½", for A1, B1, and C1

1 white solid square, 15" × 15"; cut into:

    4 rectangles, 1¼" × 3", for A2 and C2

    8 rectangles, 1¼" × 2", for A3, B2, B3, and C3

    4 rectangles, 3" × 5¾", for A4 and C4

    4 rectangles, 2½" × 5½", for A5 and C5

2 blue print rectangles, 2¾" × 4½", for C6

Paper for foundation piecing

Assembly

Press all seam allowances in the direction indicated by the arrows. Refer to "Foundation Piecing" on page 136 as needed.

1. Make one copy each of foundation patterns A–C on pattern sheet 4.

2. Sew each section in numerical order, starting with section A. Trim and press each seam as a new piece is added.

3. Trim each section, leaving a ¼" seam allowance all around each one.

4. Stitch section A to B. Press. Add section C to A/B and press. Make two sections.

5. Join the sections, rotating one section as shown and press to make a 6½" block. Carefully remove the foundation paper and press again.

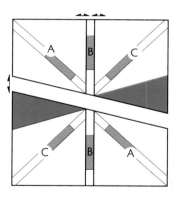

For the Love

• SHARON BURGESS •

Inspired by the beautiful tulip blooms that grace the public gardens of my home town each year—and following my own quilting mantra of create what you love— I selected one of my favorite blooms for my block. ~Sharon

What You'll Need

1 cream print square, 7" × 7", for background

1 red floral piece, 4" × 9", for A

1 red dot piece, 1½" × 9", for B

1 navy print square, 1¾" × 1¾", for C

Template plastic

Cardstock for English-paper-piecing foundations

Assembly

Refer to "English Paper Piecing" on page 136 as needed.

1. Make a template for pieces A–C using the patterns on page 129 and the template plastic. Trace the templates onto the cardstock and cut out directly on the line to make the foundations.

2. Pin the shapes to the chosen fabrics as follows and cut out, adding a generous ¼" seam allowance all around for basting.

- Red floral: 4 of piece A and 4 of piece A reverse
- Red dot: 4 of piece B
- Navy print: 1 of piece C

3. Fold the fabric seam allowance over the foundations and baste through all thicknesses.

4. Sew the A and A reverse pieces to the B piece, placing them right sides together and using a whipstitch (page 136). Make four tulip units.

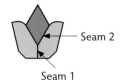

5. Sew the tulip units to the C square using a whipstitch. Press.

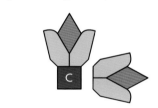

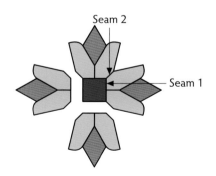

6. Apply small dots of glue around the seam allowance of the tulip and position it on the background square. Appliqué in place using a blind stitch.

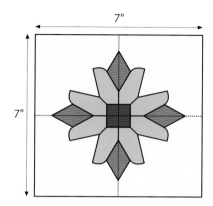

Appliqué placement guide

7. On the wrong side of the block, carefully cut away the background fabric, leaving a ¼" seam allowance. Remove the basting stitches and gently remove the paper foundations.

8. Press the block on the wrong side and trim it to 6½" square, keeping the design centered.

QUILT LAYOUTS

Starting on page 139 are several quilt layout options. Choose the one you like best, or create your own layout.

Starting on page 139 are several quilt layout options.

ALTERNATE COLORWAY

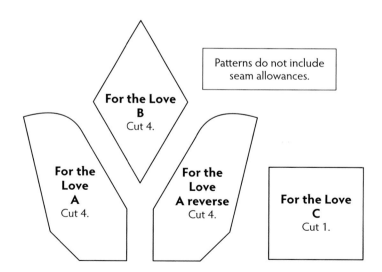

Patterns do not include seam allowances.

For the Love
B
Cut 4.

For the Love
A
Cut 4.

For the Love
A reverse
Cut 4.

For the Love
C
Cut 1.

Happy Trails

• JUDY ENGIME •

Making my first quilt at the age of 15 started an art passion that would follow me through my life's journeys. Life's trail took me to Montana, where my love for all things western grew. Any opportunity to join the two interests makes me happy! ~Judy

What You'll Need

1 blue print piece, 8" × 10";
    cut into:
    A: 44 squares, 1" × 1"
    B: 3 squares, 1½" × 1½"
1 navy floral piece, 6" × 10";
    cut into:
    C: 27 squares, 1" × 1"
    D: 3 squares, 1½" × 1½"
1 red print square, 5" × 5"; cut into:
    E: 8 squares, 1" × 1"
    F: 1 square, 1½" × 1½"
1 green print piece, 6" × 8";
    cut into:
    G: 19 squares, 1" × 1"
    H: 5 squares, 1½" × 1½"
1 yellow print piece, 6" × 10";
    cut into:
    I: 31 squares, 1" × 1"
    J: 4 squares, 1½" × 1½"
Scraps of leather for horse and
    mane appliqués
Template plastic

Assembly

Press all seam allowances in the direction indicated by the arrows.

1. Draw a diagonal line from corner to corner on the wrong side of the B and H squares.

2. Referring to "Triangle Squares" on page 137, place a B square on a D square with right sides together. Sew, cut, and press to make two half-square-triangle units. Trim the units to measure 1" square. Make six.

Make 6.

3. Repeat step 2 using the marked H squares and the J squares to make eight half-square-triangle units. Use the remaining marked H square and the F square to make two half-square-triangle units. You'll use seven H/J units. Discard or save one unit for another project.

Make 8.   Make 2.

4. Lay out the A, C, E, G, and I squares along with the half-square-triangle units in 12 rows. Sew the pieces into rows and press. Join the rows and press. The block should measure 6½" square.

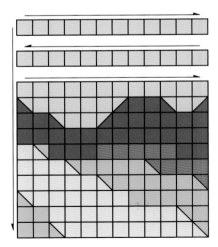

5. Trace the horse and mane patterns below onto template plastic. Cut out the shapes directly on the line. Use the template to then cut out one horse and one mane from leather. Clip both long sides of the mane, making 12 to 15 clips on each side, to make a fringe. Note that the clips on the left side are shorter than the ones on the right side; be sure to leave about ¼" unclipped between the two sides.

6. Position the horse on the 7" background square. Straight stitch around the edges to secure. Place the mane on the horse and stitch down the unclipped section.

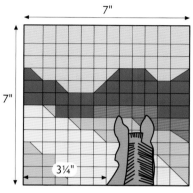

Appliqué placement guide

7. Trim the completed block to 6½" square.

SEW WHAT YOU LOVE

Making 100 blocks can be overwhelming at first. Flip through the book and place a sticky note on the blocks that capture your attention. Start with the blocks you love.

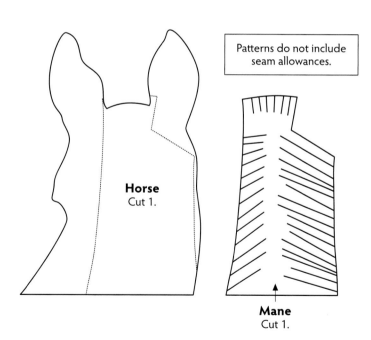

Patterns do not include seam allowances.

Horse
Cut 1.

Mane
Cut 1.

Comfort Food

• JANE DAVIDSON •

When I'm in a creative frenzy and working day and night to finish a project, I get cravings for ice cream—pistachio or French vanilla with strawberries. There's nothing like devouring a bowl of ice cream to comfort the soul. ~Jane

What You'll Need

1 cream print rectangle, 2¼" × 3½", for A1

1 red stripe rectangle, 1" × 3½", for A2

1 green print #1 piece, 7" × 11", cut into:

    2 rectangles, 1¼" × 2", for A3 and A4

    1 rectangle, 1½" × 3½", for A5

    2 squares, 5" × 5", for B2 and B3

1 green print #2 piece, 5" × 9", cut into:

    2 rectangles, 2½" × 3¾", for A6 and A7

    1 rectangle, 1¼" × 7", for B4

1 yellow print square, 4" × 4", for B1

Scrap of red and green prints for strawberry and strawberry top

Paper for foundation piecing

Template plastic or freezer paper

Appliqué glue

Dark green embroidery floss

Assembly

Press all seam allowances in the direction indicated by the arrows. Refer to "Foundation Piecing" on page 136 as needed. The instructions are written for needle-turn appliqué. Reverse the strawberry patterns for fusible appliqué.

1. Make one copy of each foundation pattern on page 133.

2. Sew each section in numerical order, starting with section A. Trim and press each seam as a new piece is added.

3. Trim around each section along the outer lines, which includes a ¼" seam allowance.

4. Stitch section A to B. Press to make a 6½" block. Carefully remove the foundation paper and press again.

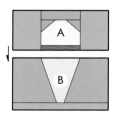

5. Make templates from plastic or freezer paper using the strawberry patterns on page 133. Trace around the templates onto the right side of the chosen fabrics. Cut out, adding a scant ¼" seam allowance all around.

6. Referring to the photo, position the pieces on the block and pin or baste in place. Stitch by hand using a blind stitch.

7. Embroider the strawberry top using two strands of embroidery floss and straight stitches. See "Embroidery Stitches" on page 138 for stitching instructions.

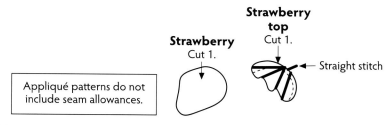

Strawberry
Cut 1.

Strawberry top
Cut 1.

← Straight stitch

Appliqué patterns do not include seam allowances.

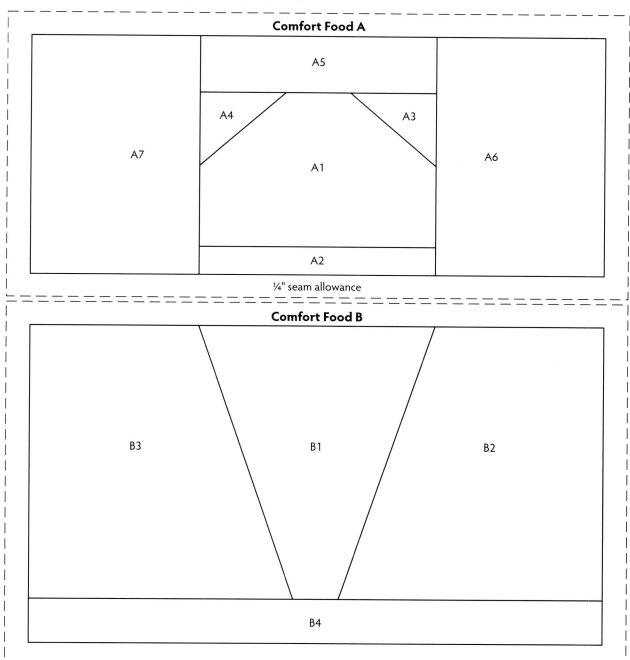

Comfort Food A

A5

A4

A3

A7

A1

A6

A2

¼" seam allowance

Comfort Food B

B3

B1

B2

B4

Make 1 copy of each.

If the construction techniques used in the blocks are unfamiliar, here you'll find the basic information you need.

Appliqué

The instructions for each block state the appliqué method used by the designer. To convert between fusible and needle-turn appliqué, you may need to reverse the patterns. Seam allowances are not included on the appliqué patterns unless noted. You'll need to add them for needle-turn appliqué patterns.

For machine appliqué, use a stabilizer on the back to support dense machine stitching (such as satin stitching) and to keep the fabric from tunneling. Choose a stabilizer that matches the weight of the fabric. After the appliqué is complete, gently remove the stabilizer.

FUSIBLE APPLIQUÉ

Raw-edged appliqué using paper-backed fusible web is a fast and easy way to appliqué. Because appliqué designs are drawn on the paper side of the fusible web, and then flipped when ironed onto the fabric, you may need to reverse the appliqué patterns prior to tracing the designs. (We have indicated where patterns have already been reversed.) Add ¼" underlap allowance to those edges that lie under another appliqué shape.

Trace the pattern pieces, also drawing the needed underlap allowances, on the paper side of the fusible web, leaving at least ½" between all the pieces. Cut about ¼" outside each drawn line.

To eliminate stiffness in pieces larger than 1", you can cut out the center of the fusible web ¼" inside the drawn line, making a ring of fusible web.

Following the manufacturer's directions, iron the web, paper side up, to the wrong side of the fabric. Cut out the shape exactly on the drawn line. Carefully

pull away the paper backing. Fuse the pieces to the background as shown in the placement diagram for the block you're making.

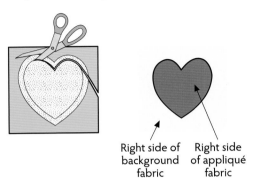

Right side of background fabric   Right side of appliqué fabric

To finish the raw edges, stitch by machine using a satin stitch, zigzag stitch, or blanket stitch and matching or invisible thread.

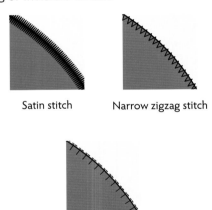

Satin stitch   Narrow zigzag stitch

Blanket stitch

You can also stitch by hand using a blanket stitch.

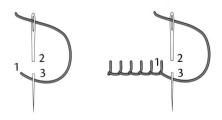

Blanket stitch

NEEDLE-TURN APPLIQUÉ

For this method of appliqué, it's helpful to cut your appliqué pieces so the bias edges are on the perimeter. This makes the edges easier to turn under and stitch smoothly in place. Trace the pattern onto freezer paper or template plastic and cut on the drawn line to make a template. Place the template face up on the right side of the fabric and lightly draw around it (place the template face down on the right side to reverse the appliqué). Cut out each appliqué about ¼" outside the marked line.

Pin or baste the appliqués on the background fabric. Stitch in place, using your needle to turn under the seam allowances as you stitch. On inward curves, clip the seam allowance almost to the marked seamline to make turning the edge easier.

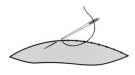

Appliqué stitch

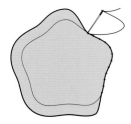

If the background fabric shows through the appliqué, carefully cut away the background fabric to within ¼" of the stitching after appliquéing the shape in place. Another option is to use two layers of appliqué fabric to prevent show-through.

Bias Strips

Bias strips are cut at a 45° angle to the straight grain of the fabric. They are stretchy and therefore ideal for creating curved appliqué stems.

Make the first cut by aligning a 45° guideline on your acrylic ruler with the cut edge or selvage of the fabric. Use this new bias edge to cut strips the required width.

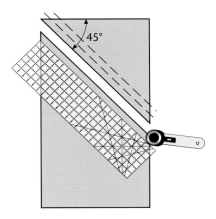

Prepare bias strips for appliqué by folding them in half lengthwise, wrong sides together. Stitch ¼" from the raw edges. Trim the seam allowances to ⅛". Center the seam allowance on the wrong side and press. A bias pressing bar is helpful for this.

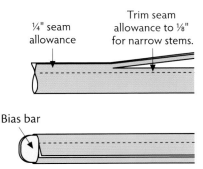

Curved Piecing

Cut pieces using a small-bladed rotary cutter or trace the templates and use scissors to maneuver the curves. Make short clips into the concave seam allowance to help with pinning and sewing.

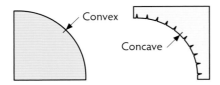

With right sides together, pin the convex piece to the inside curve (concave) of the second piece at the middle, the ends, and a few places in between. Sew with the concave piece on top, stopping frequently with the needle down to adjust the fabric so it lies flat under the needle and presser foot. After stitching, press the seam allowances toward the convex piece.

English Paper Piecing

With this method, the fabric pieces are basted around a stiff piece of paper (cardstock), and then the edges of the prepared pieces are whipstitched together.

Trace and cut a piece of stiff paper for each piece in the design. Place the paper template on the wrong side of the chosen fabric and pin it in place. Cut around the shape, adding a generous ¼" seam allowance all around.

Fold the seam allowance over the edge of the paper template and hold in place. With needle and thread, baste the seam allowance through all thicknesses with long stitches. When you reach the end of the first side, fold over the next seam allowance

and continue stitching. Continue in this manner, making sharp folds at each corner, until all the seam allowances are basted in place. For some shapes, the folding will create tails; leave the tails hanging out as shown. Backstitch at the end to secure the stitches. Repeat for each piece needed.

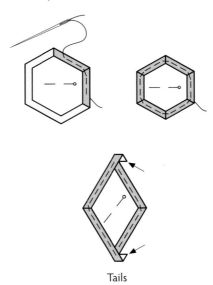

Tails

To assemble the block, place the pieces right sides together. With a single strand of thread, whipstitch them together from corner to corner, catching only the folded edges. Repeat to join all pieces. When all edges have been joined, clip the basting threads and remove them from each piece as instructed with each block. Carefully pull out the paper templates. You can reuse the templates.

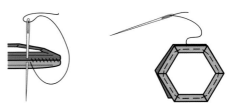

Foundation Piecing

Make paper copies of each foundation as required for the chosen block. Sew pieces to the foundation in numerical order. Center the first fabric under space #1, with the wrong side of the fabric against the unprinted side of the paper. The piece should extend beyond the seam allowances on all sides. Pin in place from the paper side.

Turn the piece with the fabric side up. Using a piece of fabric sufficient to cover space #2 and its seam allowances, position piece #2 right sides together on piece #1 as shown, aligning the edges to be sewn. The edge of the piece should extend at least ¼" into the space #2 area. Pin in place.

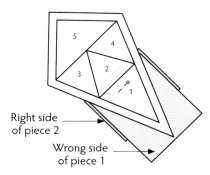

Right side of piece 2

Wrong side of piece 1

Set your sewing machine for a very short stitch length (18–20 stitches per inch or 1.5 mm). Turn the unit paper side up. Stitch through the paper and the fabric layers along the printed seamline, beginning and ending ¼" beyond the ends of the line.

Turn the unit to the fabric side. Trim the seam allowances to approximately ¼". Press so that space #2 is covered.

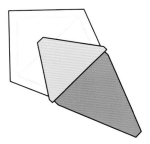

Repeat this process to complete the blocks or sections, allowing at least ¼" of fabric to extend beyond the edge of the paper. Use a rotary cutter and ruler to trim ¼" outside the seamline of the foundation, creating the seam allowance. The printed foundation patterns include the outer seam allowances, so you'll be trimming on the outer lines. Once all the seams around a foundation have been sewn, carefully remove the paper foundation.

Triangle Squares

With right sides together and the lighter fabric on top, layer one square of each color as instructed for the block you're making. On the lighter square, draw a diagonal line from corner to corner. You may draw the diagonal line before or after layering the squares. Stitch ¼" from both sides of the line. Cut apart on the marked line.

With the darker fabric on top, open out the top piece and press. Trim the dog-ear points at the corners. Each pair of squares will yield two identical half-square-triangle units.

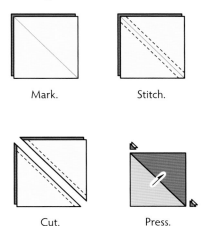

Mark.   Stitch.

Cut.   Press.

Stitch and Flip

Align a square on a corner of a larger square, a rectangle, or a pieced unit as directed in the block instructions. Mark a diagonal line on the square from corner to corner. You may have already drawn this line; just make sure you place it slanting in the correct direction. Sew on the marked line. Trim the seam allowances to ¼" as shown. Flip the resulting triangle open and press.

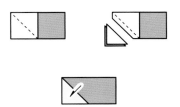

Embroidery Basics

Hand embroidery requires very little in the way of special tools. It's time-honored hand sewing that anyone can do. Using a hoop to stitch is optional. You'll need a small one, about 4" in diameter, for the blocks in this book. Try stitching without one; if you're happy with the results, don't worry about a hoop.

BASIC EMBROIDERY SUPPLIES

Here's what you'll need for the embroidered blocks:

- Large-eye embroidery needle
- Embroidery floss, heavy thread, or pearl cotton
- Pencil or water-soluble fabric marker
- Water-soluble embroidery stabilizer (optional)
- Light box (optional)
- Small hoop (optional)

TRANSFERRING THE DESIGN

The simplest way to transfer the embroidery design is to trace it directly onto the background fabric with a water-soluble marking pen. Some people mark lightly with a very sharp or mechanical pencil or a Pigma pen, later covering these marks with their stitching. To help see the design, use a light box or tape the pattern and fabric to a sunny window. You can also use a water-soluble stabilizer, tracing the design onto the stabilizer first. Adhere the stabilizer to the background fabric, stitch the design through it, and then remove the stabilizer by soaking the piece in water. Look for this product in shops that sell other needlework supplies and follow the manufacturer's instructions.

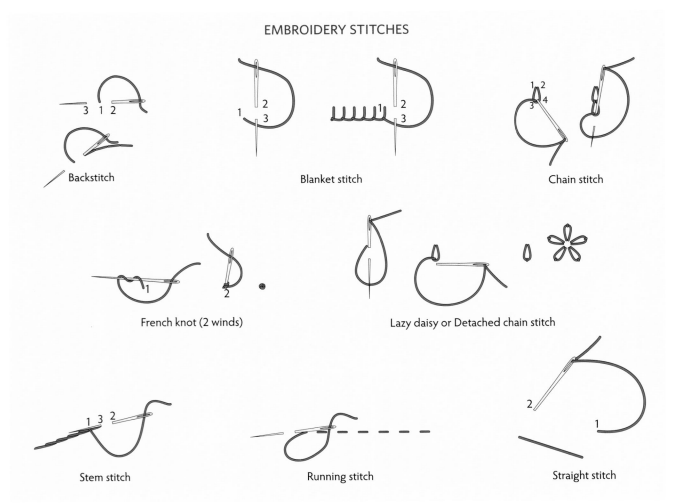

EMBROIDERY STITCHES

Backstitch

Blanket stitch

Chain stitch

French knot (2 winds)

Lazy daisy or Detached chain stitch

Stem stitch

Running stitch

Straight stitch

100 Blocks + 1 • **72½" × 72½"**

Designed and pieced by Jane Davidson and Pat Sloan and quilted by Jane Davidson.
For full instructions on making this quilt, visit ShopMartingale.com/SplendidSampler2.

Heart and Hands • **52½" × 56½"**

Designed by Pat Sloan, pieced by Melanie Barrett, and quilted by Shelley Pagliai.
For full instructions on making this quilt, visit ShopMartingale.com/SplendidSampler2.

Nine Patch Dance ▪ 25½" × 25½"

Designed, pieced, and quilted by Susan Ache.

For full instructions on making this quilt, visit ShopMartingale.com/SplendidSampler2.

Lovin' the Blues • 30" × 50"

Designed, pieced, and quilted by Tammy Vonderschmitt.

For full instructions on making this quilt, visit ShopMartingale.com/SplendidSampler2.

BLOCK INDEX

Meet Jane Davidson

I have a love affair with quilting. I have always been a bit of a crafty person, and I can honestly say I wake up every morning happy in the fact that I love what I do: designing, publishing, long-arm quilting, and teaching. Designing is my favorite part of the quilting experience, and I jump at the opportunity to make an original pattern for a magazine or book. Visit me at QuiltJane.com to see what's new.

Meet Pat Sloan

I'm a quilt designer, author, teacher, radio/podcast show producer and host, and fabric designer. My passion for making quilts, sharing quilts, and talking with quilters is limitless. I travel to teach and I host several Internet groups of quilters where we share on a daily basis what we make. I also write about quilting on my website. To find me, go to PatSloan.com, sign up for my newsletter, and let's chat soon!